100 Years Ago

The Glorious 1890's

GALLERY BOOKS
An Imprint of W.H. Smith Publishers Inc.
112 Madison Avenue
New York City 10016

100 Years Ago

The Glorious 1890s

Diana Claitor

(PREVIOUS PAGES) The Silver Cornet Band of Moro, Oregon, was in step with the times when it played popular tunes like the Washington Post March by John Philip Sousa.

An M & M Book

Copyright 1990 by M & M Books

ISBN 0-8317-6552-6

100 Years Ago: The Glorious 1890s was prepared and produced by Moore & Moore Publishing, 11 W. 19th Street, New York, N.Y. 10011

Project Director & Editor Gary Fishgall

Photo Research Maxine Dormer, Jana Marcus, Janice Ostan, Lucinda Stellini

Senior Editorial Assistant Shirley Vierheller; Editorial Assistants Maxine Dormer, David Blankenship, Ben D'Amprisi, Jr., Ben McLaughlin, Sarah Boyar, Lisa Pike; Copy Editor Phil Alkana

Designer Michael Harvey

Separations and Printing Regent Publishing Services Ltd.

Typesetting Dynographics, Inc.

First published in the United States in 1990 by Gallery Books, an imprint of W.H. Smith Publishers, Inc., 112 Madison Avenue, New York, New York 10016

Gallery Books are available for bulk purchase for sales promotions and premium use. For details write or telephone the Manager of Special Sales, W.H. Smith Publishers, Inc., 112 Madison Avenue, New York, New York 10016. (212) 532-6600

CONTENTS

*In a sylvan Florida setting, eight gents and ladies form
a tableau that is a fitting portrait of the "Gilded Age."*

Introduction

A people without history is like the wind on the buffalo grass.
A Sioux expression

It was the age of Enrico Caruso, Lillian Russell, and William Frederick Cody. Of Marie Curie, William McKinley, and Peter Ilyich Tchaikovsky. It was a time when the automobile and the steel-frame skyscraper were born, the Wild West came to an end, and America emerged from the worst economic depression in 20 years to become a world power. Today it is best remembered as the "Gilded Age," an era when individuals like J. P. Morgan and Andrew Carnegie were amassing vast fortunes unimpeded by income taxes, but it was also the age of one of the largest mass migrations in history, when millions of immigrants sought freedom and opportunity in America as a refuge from oppression abroad.

These were the 1890s, the last decade of the 19th century, 100 years ago. America was very different then. The airplane was a decade away from creation. There were no forms of mass communication, although Marconi's invention of the wireless and Edison's invention of the moving picture during the decade would bring the world closer to that eventuality. Even the telephone and the electric light were just beginning to affect daily life. Moreover, at the decade's outset, the Indian Wars still persisted, very few women worked outside the home, and, for the most part, the man ruled the Victorian household as a benevolent despot.

As we stand on the brink of the 21st century, it seems somehow fitting that we should look back at the equivalent moment of the last century. In so doing, we find that the 1890s were a watershed decade, a crucial dividing line for our nation, both culturally and politically. During the decade, the United States progressed from a primarily agricultural economy to one that was largely industrial, from a rural society of self-reliant folk with large extended families to an urban society of interdependent strangers, and from a country seeking to fulfill its "manifest destiny" across the North American continent to a nation with an international outlook. Surprisingly, the transformations wrought 100 years ago are still affecting the nation today.

To be sure, life in the 1890s was exciting, eventful—and, yes, even glorious. At the same time, it was a complex decade, and not entirely pleasant. Of course, it is not possible to capture all those complexities in this informal history of 192 pages, yet it is possible to illuminate many of the more important aspects of the era.

In selecting the photographs and subjects for *100 Years Ago: The Glorious 1890s*, we have sought to focus on as broad a range as possible—from the Spanish-American War to women working in factories to Butch Cassidy and the Sundance Kid. Some of the stories, like those covering the Boer War, the case of *Plessey* v. *Ferguson*, and the burgeoning city reform movement reverbate with issues and events that significantly affected life well into the 20th century. Others, like those on the Sears, Roebuck catalog and the era's penchant for cluttered interiors, focus on transitory, yet charming aspects of life in this bygone age.

As we look at the images in this volume, the considerable differences between the customs of the 1890s and those of the 1990s become apparent: courting men and women sit at a formal distance from one another, the family out for a Sunday drive in the country is dressed quite grandly, some of the factory workers are very young children.

On the other hand, one can find surprising similarities between the America of the 1890s and the America of today. As we look into the uncertain eyes of an immigrant child just off the boat in 1895, we can see the same hopes and fears of present-day immigrants who arrive by air. The soldiers marching off to glory in Cuba in 1897 have an air of patriotic bravado very much like American soldiers in our current "splendid little wars." The same pride of ownership that marks a family with its first phonograph now accompanies the aquisition of a VCR or a PC.

There are, in fact, some uncanny parallels linking the 1890s to the 1990s: during the former America changed from an agrarian to an industrial society, whereas during the latter we are witnessing the nation's transformation from a manufacturing to a high-tech society. The current surge toward capitalist and democratic ideals around the globe seems to echo the enormous growth of America's influence in the world community 100 years ago. Fears about working mothers and the degeneration of the family are common to both eras, but so too is a sense of optimism and patriotism.

Above all, this backward glance reminds us that 100 years ago is not so very long in many respects. We are still a nation of immigrants and a nation of idealists. As we move toward a new century and an unknown future, it is useful to see ourselves as we looked at the last turn of a century—when Americans were riding high, wide, and handsome, unafraid of what lay ahead.

THE WINDS OF CHANGE

The Winds of Change

The United States—and indeed the world—did a lot of growing up in the 1890s. It was a decade of change that hinted at even greater change to come. And when the decade ended, the signposts of the modern age were considerably more visible than they had been ten years earlier.

It was a decade of new ideas. The third volume of Karl Marx's *Das Kapital* was published; Freud began his ground-breaking work in psychoanaylysis, publishing *Studies on Hysteria* with his partner Josef Breur in 1895; and Theodor Herzl organized the first international Zionist congress in 1897, with the goal of establishing a Jewish state in Palestine.

It was a decade of exploding technology. The first automobile was built, and the first moving pictures were shown. Experimental aircraft was tested, and long-distance phone lines were laid. The German physicist Wilhelm Roentgen discovered the X ray and Madame Curie identified radium and polonium.

It was a decade of changing political fortunes, too. The Democrats won and then lost the U.S. presidency. William Gladstone became prime minister of Great Britain, and Kaiser Wilhelm II of Germany dismissed his chancellor, Otto von Bismarck, architect of the modern German nation. Russia, on the brink of one of the greatest revolutions in history, saw Nicholas II, the last Tsar, mount the throne in 1894. China, already in disarray due to the

The Haynes gas-powered auto, 1893.

The founder of psychoanalysis, Sigmund Freud.

encroachment of Western powers, endured a humiliating defeat in 1895 at the hands of Japan.

But through it all, there was the one constant: a small and indomitable figure, Queen Victoria of England, who celebrated her Diamond Jubilee in 1897. Yet, even in the midst of this island of stability, the Boer War in South Africa signaled change. The beginning of the end of the British Empire lay on the horizon while, at almost the same time, the Spanish-American War marked the beginning of the age of America. Indeed, the 1890s saw the United States awakening to a sense of its own power. By the dawn of the 20th century, it was no longer possible to view the United States as an offshoot of Western Europe.

When the decade began, there were few signs of what lay ahead. The Republican President Benjamin Harrison was a lackluster leader who had done little more than reform the civil service during his term of office. And out

(PREVIOUS PAGES) *Col. Theodore Roosevelt and his Rough Riders receive a rousing welcome home after their stirring victory at San Juan Hill, Cuba, during the Spanish-American War.*

West, farmers, indebted to the Eastern mortgage companies and the railroads, were failing at an unprecedented rate. But from the seeds of their discontent sprang a new political force, the Populist Party.

The hero of the Populists was the famous orator from Lincoln, Nebraska, William Jennings Bryan, who believed that government's reliance on the gold standard was crippling the small businessmen and farmers. Bryan would become the Democratic Party's standard-bearer three times, beginning in 1896, but prior to his first run for the presidency, the Populists helped Democrat Grover Cleveland reclaim the Oval Office in 1893. Cleveland, who first served as president from 1885 to 1889, did not enjoy a happy second term. Just two months after his inauguration, the Panic of 1893 struck and the United States was plunged into the worst economic depression in two decades.

After the stock market crashed, President Cleveland desperately sought to stop the depletion of the nation's gold reserves, which were sinking to an all time low. In desperation, he turned to financial titan J. P. Morgan. Morgan's banking syndicate, linked with railroads, utilities, and insurance companies, controlled enormous chunks of America's wealth. His bank arranged the necessary bond sales that saved the U.S. economy. It was probably the only time in American history that one private individual single-handedly rescued the nation from financial ruin. Many Americans, unfairly or not, blamed Cleveland for the crisis and saw his collaboration with Morgan as a betrayal.

Four million unemployed may have walked the streets, but amid the confusion and the despair of the mid-1890s, a new spirit of optimism and nationalism was born. Republican President William McKinley took office in 1897 and quickly adapted to this spirit, presiding over the Spanish-American War and the annexation of the United

Financier and philanthropist John Pierpont Morgan, Sr.

States' first foreign possessions, Guam and the Philippines in 1898. With the rest of his party, McKinley believed the United States should develop an empire in the old British style and for the same reasons: to create markets for American products and to Christianize the natives. The American public's enthusiasm for the war was fueled by a sensation-seeking press, led by publisher William Randolph Hearst, which used inflammatory rhetoric to increase the readership of its newspapers.

The enthusiasm for action overseas did not carry over to internal reform. During this decade, the movements to expand the rights of women and blacks faltered temporarily, although several of the new Western states gave women the right to vote, and some progress was made in extending higher education and business opportunities to the blacks. It was in the 1890s, however, that American women began to develop a distinct persona. In *Life* magazine, the popular Gibson Girl wore streamlined clothes and was shown bicycling and playing tennis, activities considered revolutionary for a woman at the time. Women and men alike found a new heroine in 25-year-old journalist Nellie Bly, who set a new speed record when she travelled around the world alone in 72 days for her newspaper, the *New York World*.

The journey of Nellie Bly also served to remind Americans of their place in an increasingly interdependent world. The nation was changing directions: from isolationism to expansionism and from a rural orientation to one that was predominantly urban. Some citizens yearned for the good old days when America was more insular and countrified, but most welcomed progress. The average American liked electric lights, telephones, and trains that roared across the landscape. He believed it right and inevitable that the United States establish its dominion over other cultures. It was the 1890s, and America was ready to take her place on the world stage.

Newspaper publisher and political candidate William Randolph Hearst

Three U.S. presidents faced widely-varying problems during the roller coaster ride of 1890s politics . . .

(RIGHT) *Republican Benjamin Harrison, a man of intelligence and independence, was both preceded and succeeded by Grover Cleveland. Harrison is remembered for his focus on the economic problems of the day, and especially for the groundbreaking Sherman Antitrust Act of 1890, which outlawed the trusts and monopolies that inhibited open trade.*

(BELOW) *William McKinley had a presidential bearing that made his campaign appearances from the back of a train all the more effective. Foreign policy concerns, including the Spanish-American War, dominated his presidency, which extended from 1896 to his assassination in 1901.*

(OPPOSITE) *The second inauguration of Democrat Grover Cleveland in 1893. Cleveland's administration was marked by discord and disappointment, due in part to the nation's economic and labor troubles and in part to the president's disagreement with his party over the repeal of the silver laws.*

GENTLEMEM OUR COUNTRY

(ABOVE) *Henry Ford's first auto appeared three years after that of the Duryeas. Early designers publicized their models by competing in speed trials, which stirred the public's enthusiasm for the odd looking machines. As this photo illustrates, Ford also used patriotism.*

(RIGHT) *The Duryea automobile, the first successful gasoline-powered auto in America, grew out of the experiments of Charles and J. Frank Duryea, a pair of brothers who were bicycle mechanics. Their two-cycle, one-cylinder car first appeared in 1893.*

One Woman, One Vote

Even before the Civil War, they were agitating for the right to vote, the right known as suffrage. But by the 1890s the determined women known as suffragettes faced increasingly vocal opposition ... from other women. These antisuffragists, often socially prominent ladies, believed that voting would naturally lead females into politics and then destroy the family. Extremists also predicted that if allowed to vote, women would become "large-handed, big-footed, flat-chested and thin-lipped."

Besides fears like these, 40 years of mostly unsuccessful efforts had slowed the movement's momentum, as had divisions within its leadership. Moreover, changing social and economic conditions, including the Panic of 1893, drew attention away from the issue of women's rights and placed it on more immediate concerns, such as food and shelter.

Still the suffragettes had reason to cheer. After all, 1890 saw Wyoming enter the Union as the first state with full voting rights for women. And Colorado, Utah, and Idaho would enfranchise women before the century's close.

Progress was to follow on other fronts as well. Since 1848, when New York State had given married women domain over their own property, other legal rights had been granted to females. Some were able to become doctors and lawyers. These victories were due in large measure to Elizabeth Cady Stanton and Susan B. Anthony, two remarkably different women who lobbied, spoke, and wrote tirelessly on behalf of women's rights. "I forged the thunderbolts and she fired them," said Stanton of their partnership.

Stanton and Anthony, who built the National Women Suffrage Association, firmly believed in working toward a national voting rights amendment, but the less militant Woman Suffrage Association led by Lucy Stone and Henry Ward Beecher concentrated on state campaigns. In 1890, the two factions merged in the National American Woman Suffrage Association and over time Stone's philosophy gradually prevailed. But Stanton remained the queen—and a major spokesperson—of the women's movement until her death in 1902.

Despite the dramatic differences in their personalities, Susan B. Anthony (left) and Elizabeth Cady Stanton made a dynamic team in the ongoing fight for women's rights in the 1890s.

An increasing range of colors and the use of a variety of materials brought attractive fashions to the 1890s . . .

A Tallahassee, Florida, cleric with a full beard (left) and with just a moustache (right), signalling a change in the preferred style of men's facial hair.

Sporty gentlemen began to dress in shorter jackets and wore black top hats in the evening, while males from every strata of society boasted imaginative combinations of moustaches, sideburns, and beards. By the end of the decade, the lace-up shoe began to replace the boot as the footwear of choice.

 Children of both sexes were dressed as miniature adults.

 Long-waisted dresses with leg-of-mutton sleeves and simpler skirts made women's fashions less fussy for the most part; still, top wear could become outrageous when taken to the extreme of the balloon sleeve, as seen in the center photograph. All ages and genders wore hats.

"The Splendid Little War"

When the Spanish-American War began in early 1898, the United States was enthusiastic. Parades and parties marked the troop departures, and the men sang "There'll Be a Hot Time in the Old Town Tonight" as they boarded ships for Cuba. The battle cry "Remember the *Maine*" was on everyone's lips and war fever was in the air.

During the preceding years, the yellow journalism of the Hearst and Pulitzer newspapers had helped fan antagonism for the brutal Spanish government in Cuba. Then came the mysterious explosion on February 15, 1898, that destroyed the U.S. battleship *Maine*, berthed in Havana harbor, and with it the lives of 260 Americans. That event, coupled with the discovery of a Spanish diplomat's insulting remarks about President William McKinley, pushed the Congress to declare war.

Almost immediately, a U.S. squadron destroyed the Spanish vessels at Manila in the Philippines. Nearly 400 Spanish sailors were killed or wounded while the American ships and men suffered only scratches. Back home, the American public cheered happily. Few realized how different—and devastating—the campaign would be in Cuba, which the American army planned to liberate from its Spanish occupiers.

Despite poor planning and organization, America's Cuban campaign went well at first, and war correspondents told of heroic battles like the one for San Juan Hill, where future president Colonel Teddy Roosevelt led his Rough Riders to victory. But war frenzy faded as malaria, dysentery, typhoid, and yellow fever killed between 2,000 and 3,000 Americans and left most of the other soldiers emaciated and ill. Nevertheless, the feeble resistance of the Spanish armed forces ended after less than four months of fighting and a peace agreement was signed on August 12, 1898. The United States was free to take possession of the islands of Guam, the Philippines, and Puerto Rico, while establishing considerable influence over the newly independent Cubans. And thus America the global power was born.

The U.S. victory in what was dubbed "the splendid little war" was partly due to the enthusiasm and skill of its forces, but it was also a reflection of luck and Spanish incompetence. As war correspondent Richard Harding Davis said, "God takes care of drunken men, sailors, and the United States."

(ABOVE LEFT) *Cuban insurgents in Villa Clara, Cuba, pose for a stereoptican cameraman.*

(ABOVE RIGHT) *Col. Teddy Roosevelt (center) with his famous Rough Riders, after defeating Spanish troops in the battle for San Juan Heights.*

(OPPOSITE) *The wreck of the U.S.S.* Maine *in Havana harbor.*

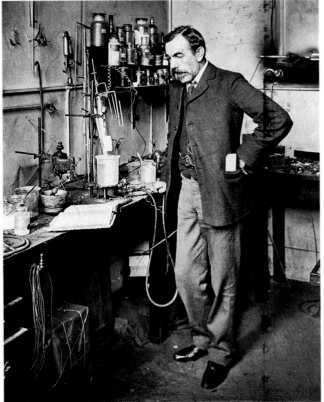

In western Europe, the 1890s saw the emergence of new insights, inventions, and innovations . . .

 (ABOVE LEFT) *The German aeronautical engineer Otto Lilienthal pioneered early heavier-than-air flying machines.*

 (ABOVE RIGHT) *Sir William Ramsay, a Scottish chemist, discovered helium and argon in his experiments with inert gases.*

 (RIGHT) *Italian physicist Guglielmo Marconi experimented with radio signals across the British Channel.*

 (ABOVE LEFT) *In 1892, William Gladstone became prime minister of England for the fourth and final time. He was forced to resign in 1894 during the controversy over home rule for Ireland.*

 (ABOVE CENTER) *Hungarian journalist Theodor Herzl, the founder of modern Zionism, advocated the creation of a Jewish state.*

 (ABOVE RIGHT) *The last tsar of Russia, Nicholas II, assumed the throne in 1894.*

(LEFT) *Polish scientist Marie Curie, in partnership with her husband Pierre, isolated radium and polonium.*

Domestics sweep the yard of a white employer in Belton, South Carolina, in 1899.

Separation and Urbanization

Homer Plessy was seven-eighth's white and very light-skinned, but in 1892, the one-eighth was what counted in the South. When he sat down in a white coach on a Louisiana train, he was told he had to move to a "colored" car. Plessy refused and was arrested, triggering a Supreme Court case that was to change almost every aspect of daily life in America.

The decision of the court in 1896 held that the events on the Louisiana train did not violate Plessy's civil rights as long as the "colored" car to which he was forced to move was of comparable quality to the white accommodation. In other words, separation of the races did not necessarily mean discrimination according to America's highest court. From that decision came a system of separate rest rooms, water fountains, parks, prisons, train cars, and schools that persisted until another Supreme Court ruling in 1954.

The case of *Plessy* v. *Ferguson* seemed to put the federal stamp of approval on the growing discrimination against African-Americans. Since the 1880s, their voting rights in Southern states had been eroded by Jim Crow laws as violence against them escalated. In 1892, 161 African-Americans were lynched by mobs. Riots, like the one in Wilmington, North Carolina, in 1898, resulted in white and black fatalities. Life wasn't much better in the North, where African-Americans were increasingly excluded from skilled trades, unions, and many public facilities. In both regions, writers and speakers openly promoted the view that blacks were less industrious, less thrifty, and less trustworthy than Caucasians.

African-Americans nonetheless tried various solutions to the "race problem" during the 1890s. The well-known educator Booker T. Washington emphasized the importance of trade schools, racial solidarity, and economic advancement, believing that if his people achieved middle-class status, they would be accorded equal rights. Others believed that the situation called for organized protest, and a few groups espoused the idea of all-black communities and even emigration from the United States.

A parallel development during the decade, sparked by the increasing presence of blacks in urban centers, resulted in the establishment of African-American businesses—insurance companies, newspapers, funeral parlors, and even banks—and this phenomenon, in turn, gave rise to a small middle class.

For the most part, however, this was the bleakest period for African-Americans since the 1850s. Although slavery had been outlawed for decades, equality between the races was a very long way off indeed.

 (RIGHT) *A lynching victim in West Virginia. More than a thousand African-Americans were hung during the decade as racial tensions in the South reached their highest level since the period preceding the Civil War.*

 (BELOW LEFT) *The Supreme Court of the U.S. in 1899. The lone dissenter in Plessy v. Ferguson, Justice John Marshall Harlan, is in the front row, second from the left. Beside him is Chief Justice Fuller.*

(BOTTOM) *The Colored Industrial Institute, Pine Bluff, Arkansas, in 1892. Schools for young black ladies at this time concentrated on teaching domestic skills.*

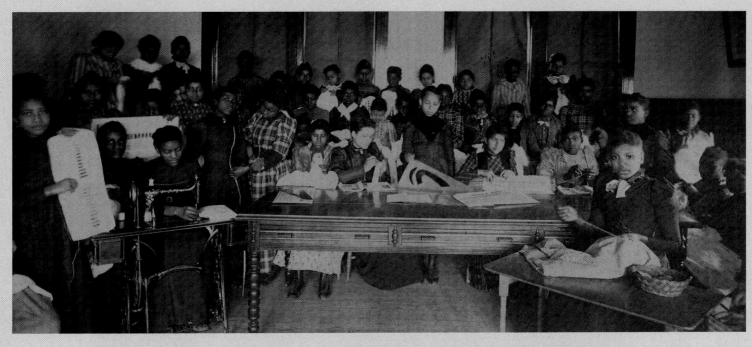

(OPPOSITE) *Queen Victoria (center) dotes on her great-grandchild, Olga, the child of her granddaughter Alexandria and Nicholas II, Czar of Russia (standing left). The heir to the British crown, Edward VII, is next to the Russian ruler.*

Almost as soon as Wilhelm II became Emperor of Germany in 1888, tensions arose between the impulsive young ruler and the powerful German chancellor, Otto von Bismarck. The latter, seen here at right with his dogs, was forced to resign in 1890. He withdrew to his estate, where he worked on his memoirs and continually criticized his successors until his death in 1898.

The Queen of an Era

The 1897 celebration of Queen Victoria's 60th year as Britain's monarch was as large and spectacular as the British empire itself. During her reign, the island nation was triumphant. Its navy ruled the world's seas and it governed more lands than had any state since Rome.

As queen, Victoria had gone from young woman to matron. She shared a happy marriage with Prince Albert and mourned his passing deeply. Her children and grandchildren would fill most of the thrones of Europe and their intrafamilial squabbles would eventually erupt into a World War.

The short, plump queen was a hard worker, but she was also a very private person and had remained almost invisible to her subjects. In 1887, she reluctantly participated in the 50th anniversary celebration of her reign, the Golden Jubilee, and she was touched by the people's affection for her. Recognizing their need to see her, she never again retreated to her former seclusion.

The much grander Diamond Jubilee was a magnificent tribute. Climaxing the festivities was an elaborate procession through the streets of London, headed by glittering waves of troops from distant colonies, in all their colorful splendor: the New Zealand mounted troops, the Borneo Dyak police, giant Maoris, diminutive Malays, turbanned lancers of the Indian empire, and numerous others, all offering dramatic proof of the strength of the empire. After the colonial troops came the British army in a sea of gold, scarlet, emerald, and blue uniforms. The carriages of royalty followed, but thousands of eyes were searching for the one special vehicle drawn by eight pale horses, and an enormous roar followed its movement toward St. Paul's Cathedral.

Every inch of space—in windows, on rooftops, and in the streets—was filled with emotional spectators who watched the small figure in black silk and a diamond and feather headpiece as she participated in the special commemorative service on the steps of the imposing cathedral.

At the dinner party at Buckingham Palace, a nine-foot-high arrangement of nearly 60,000 orchids from every corner of the empire decorated the queen's table. As she traveled back to Windsor, 10,000 school children sang the national anthem along the road. An enormous naval review at Spithead—35 miles of ships—displayed just a portion of the Royal Navy's might.

In a few years, the empire would begin to fail, but in 1897, the British people were proud of their premier status among nations. The Diamond Jubilee allowed them to express their feelings about their country—and their beloved queen.

John Wesley Hardin

William Jennings Bryan

Alexander Graham Bell

Nellie Bly

It was an era of adventure and change for America, one with a fascinating array of heroes, leaders, and villains. The public was able to read about the exploits of these colorful characters in increasingly sophisticated newspapers . . .

 Reformed gunslinger John Wesley Hardin emerged from prison as a self-taught lawyer in 1894, but he was shot down in the streets of El Paso one year later.

Alexander Graham Bell, inventor of the telephone, saw the completion of the first long-distance phone lines during the 1890s.

William Jennings Bryan's famous "Cross of Gold" speech at the 1896 Democratic national convention so impressed the delegates that the 36-year-old easily received his party's nomination for president. He was defeated in the general election by William McKinley.

Nellie Bly was an intrepid young journalist who traveled around the world in 72 days.

Lizzie Borden

Charles Dana Gibson

John Muir

Sitting Bull

The public eagerly followed the trial of Lizzie Borden, who was accused of hacking her father and stepmother to death with an axe on August 4, 1892.

Crusader John Muir changed the public's perception of conservation as he persuasively argued for the creation of national parks in books like The Mountains of California (1894).

With his drawings of stylish young ladies, Charles Dana Gibson created an entirely new personae for American women. The "Gibson Girl" was active, graceful, and modern.

Sitting Bull, a Sioux leader at the Battle of Little Big Horn (1876), was shot to death in a dispute with Indian police in 1890.

The determined Boers were mostly farmers who valued their independence above everything.

A Colonial War in Southern Africa

Although news about the Boer War filled the newspapers in the 1890s, most Americans were confused about this far-off conflict in the newly formed colonies of southern Africa. The war, which formally began in 1899, pitted the mighty British Empire against the Boers, descendants of Dutch and French settlers who lived on Africa's cape. The confusion was evident in an American soldier's letter to Colonel Teddy Roosevelt. "Dear Teddy," he wrote, "I came over here meaning to join the Boers, who I was told were Republicans fighting Monarchists; but when I got here I found the Boers talked Dutch, while the British talked English, so I joined the latter."

Mostly farmers, the Boers were a rigidly traditional people who distrusted outsiders. They had struggled long and hard to tame the rugged countryside and to subjugate its indigenous black people. But, through their perseverance, two fiercely independent republics—the Transvaal and the Orange Free state—were created.

The British had extensive commercial interests in southern Africa. For years, they and the Boers had been in conflict. Finally, the Boers declared war on the British Cape Colony, naively assuming that America, France, and Germany would come to their aid. But little help arrived, while soldiers and supplies poured into British camps from Australia, Canada, and the rest of England's colonial empire.

The war lasted 12 years, on and off. At the outset, battles were staged along formal, traditional lines; modern guerrilla warfare prevailed by the end. In a chilling presentiment of 20th century atrocities, the British placed Boer women and children in concentration camps where 20,000 of them died from epidemics. Meanwhile, the British army, nearly untested since the Napoleonic wars 84 years earlier, was revealed to be incompetent and badly organized. An overhaul came just in time for World War I. Despite the inadequacies of the British army, the Boers were no match for the mightiest nation on earth. In 1902, the war came to an end, and although the Boers became British subjects (later to regain their independence) they had taught an astonished world that a few scrappy farmers could stand against the awesome power of the British empire. And although few realized it at the time, the Boer War signaled the beginning of the end for that empire.

 These Boers, representing three generations of farmers, were photographed in 1899. They display the attire of most Boers who took the field against the British.

 British soldiers bring in a captured Afrikaner during the Boer War. Soldiers of the mighty British empire significantly outnumbered the Dutch guerillas in the prolonged conflict.

 A crowd gathers in 1898 to witness the ceremonies that marked the U.S.'s annexation of Hawaii. The acquisition resulted from years of lobbying by American business interests.

A Victim of the Times

It was a political crisis that shook France to its foundations and resulted in significant changes in the national consciousness. The Dreyfus Affair—as it was known— began with the trial of a French army captain, but over 12 years of intense public debate became a shocking expose of anti-Semitism and paranoia lurking beneath the surface of French—and indeed, Western European—society.

Alfred Dreyfus was an educated, wealthy man with a successful career in the military. He was often, however, described as cold and reserved, a perception drawn more from his position of authority and the fact that he was a Jew, than from any actual deficiencies in his personality. When the military high command learned that a German spy was in its midst, Dreyfus, who was assigned to the War Ministry, became the logical suspect despite the flimsiness of the evidence—a note penned in a handwriting similar to the captain's. Convicted of treason in 1894 and sent to Devil's Island, Dreyfus rapidly became the symbol for all "Jewish conspirators" who allegedly passed French military secrets to foreign powers.

The case revealed deep schisms in the country: divisions between supporters and detractors of the Army, between urban and country people, between tradition and modernity. On the one side, virulent newspaper articles brought together the anti-Semitic movement with political conservatives and strongly traditional Roman Catholics. On the other side were those who came to Dreyfus's defense including the novelist Emile Zola who wrote a celebrated open letter, *J'accuse* (I accuse) in which he attacked the army and stirred public sympathy for the imprisoned man.

It all seemed like a nightmare to the 34-year-old Dreyfus. Suddenly separated from a devoted wife and two children, he was publicly degraded in a ceremony removing him from the military, while an enormous crowd screamed for his head. He endured several trials and nearly five years of isolation and imprisonment on Devil's Island before he was freed in 1899. Another French officer, Ferdinand-Walsin Esterhazy, was blamed for the espionage and Dreyfus was pardoned by the President, but even then the controversy didn't fade completely. Some people simply refused to recognize the truth—that the young Frenchman had been a scapegoat and a victim of hysteria.

Alfred Dreyfus, a French Army captain accused of spying for the Germans, was arrested in 1894. He became the center of a scandal that rocked France for a decade.

MAIN STREET,
USA

Main Street, USA

Despite the growing influence of urban society in the 1890s, there were eight million farmers working the fertile lands of America. Agriculture was still the largest area of endeavor in the country. People on farms and ranches and in villages and towns disapproved of city life and many aspects of the new industrial age. They continued to work toward the goals of personal independence and modest prosperity that had traditionally defined the American dream.

There was ample evidence that the dream was coming true in the last decade of the century. Midwestern towns, which had consisted of unpainted wooden houses encircling a few struggling businesses twenty years before, were now prospering communities with elm-shaded streets, banks, business colleges, and fountains. Almost every town and village was busily establishing libraries, clubs, and societies to promote the arts, culture, and business. The men of Deadwood, North Dakota, for example, formed a Businessmen's Club in 1892, a place where respectable men could relax, eat, play cards, or discuss business. The women already sponsored several groups that were gathered together into the Black Hills Federation of Women's Clubs late in the decade. The activities of such associations were not altogether frivolous or socially oriented. One of the first efforts of the Black Hills Pioneer Society, organized in 1895, was to

The National Biscuit Company, founded in 1898, took the cracker out of the barrel and put it on the packaged goods shelf, as this Colorado store clearly illustrates.

A group of young ladies drape themselves in the Stars and Stripes, perhaps for a local pageant.

raise the requisite funds to send an indigent gentleman to a state home.

As they had in the past, religious institutions continued to play a crucial role in the lives of rural people, providing welfare and aid to those in need through numerous affiliated agencies. They also served as significant social outlets. There were the weekly religious services, of course, but there were also church-sponsored suppers, dances, and bingos. After Sunday worship, any family with a surrey or carriage would typically embark on a drive, leisurely touring the woodlands or peaceful country roads.

Although the railroad brought an increase in the amount of entertainers traveling to small-town America during the 1890s, rural leisure time still centered largely around the home. People played board games like "Electors and Presidential Puzzle," and popular instruments like the concertina, parlor organ, and above all, the piano. Long considered a requirement for the sophisticated city parlor, the piano spread to rural homes in the latter years of the 19th century.

Reading too was a primary form of entertainment, as well as a source of information. Among those catering to the rural demand for literature was Montgomery Ward, which featured a 39-page book section in its 1895 catalog. It offered classical literature, self-help books, cook-

(PREVIOUS PAGES) Dressed in their springtime finery, a group of Utah girls ready themselves for a Maypole dance.

books, even the latest best-sellers like *Peck's Bad Boy* and Rudyard Kipling's *The Jungle Book*. It also advertised discreet manuals to answer matters that were not discussed in polite society, like *The Physical Life of Women*.

Telephones were rare outside the cities and newspapers were less prevalent in rural areas, so small-town communications often centered around the general merchandise store. Here people gathered to exchange information, share ideas, and just plain gossip. The merchant himself was a clearinghouse; he knew who was sick, who was expecting a baby, and who was awaiting relatives for a visit. Sometimes the store owner was also the postmaster, and in many cases he was a leader in the church and community.

The farm family was probably the purest example of the old way of living and the ideals that gave rise to America; people were close to the land and close to each other. They were self-sufficient in many ways, too. Most farm families in the 1890s still made and did almost everything by hand, and usually the farm women performed as much of that hard work as the men. For example, Mary Larson of North Dakota had the daily job of hauling water for the oxen on her farm. To accomplish this task, she had to hitch up a horse to a wagon and drive six miles to a well. There she had to draw the water by hand—enough to fill three 60-gallon barrels on the wagon—and transport it back to the fields where her husband was ploughing.

It was often said that women suffered most from the lack of opportunities attendant to rural life, as well as the isolation and privations of such an existence. Thousands perished in childbirth for lack of rudimentary medical care. Others watched helplessly as their children died of

The catalogue published by Sears, Roebuck and Co. in 1896.

treatable ailments. As the decade grew old, it was often the mothers who encouraged their sons and daughters to seek their fortunes in the cities.

In the years following the Civil War, hundreds of thousands of people settled in America's villages and towns. The number of farms and acreage under cultivation tripled during the 19th century. By the 1890s, however, a reverse migration had set in and people began to leave the farms and small towns of America as part of a growing discontent with rural life. Those who remained were both attracted to and repulsed by the values of urban society. They desired the perfumes, silks, and labor-saving devices that they could order from the cities of the East, but to afford these luxuries they had to be willing to raise certain kinds of crops—cash crops—and to pay high prices to ship those crops to market. To those who made the accommodation, rural life lost some of its bucolic charm and the independent people of America's towns, villages, and countryside became—or so it seemed to them—cogs in the industrial machine. As the century drew to a close, these folks hung on to the best of the old ways and tried to incorporate the new. It was a time of adaptation for Main Street, USA.

A farmer carefully makes an entry in his ledger book.

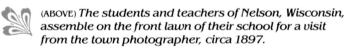

(ABOVE) *The students and teachers of Nelson, Wisconsin, assemble on the front lawn of their school for a visit from the town photographer, circa 1897.*

(LEFT) *Churches were among the principal social institutions in small-town America during the 1890s. This typical New England sideboard was the Old West Church in Calais, Vermont.*

School was conducted in a formal atmosphere in the 1890s, with education consisting primarily of copying, memorization, and recitation.

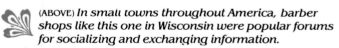

(ABOVE) *In small towns throughout America, barber shops like this one in Wisconsin were popular forums for socializing and exchanging information.*

(LEFT) *This watering hole in Tallahassee, Florida, was known as Mr. Jacobs' bar. The proprietor is on the left toasting with his patrons.*

(RIGHT) *For those who made the family clothes, the piece goods counter was the focal point of this New England country store. But to get to it, they had to bypass the display of seeds, buckets, and sleds.*

(BELOW) *The company store in Sunrise, Wyoming, was as well-stocked and tidy as most city stores in 1895.*

Travelling salesmen and farm families enjoying a rare night in town could sample the cuisine at the Saddle Rock Restaurant in Ogden, Utah.

(OPPOSITE) *In Oklahoma City, it was possible to satisfy even the most insatiable sweet tooth on Main Street.*

The Family Farm

In the 1890s an increasingly urban America turned away from its idealistic view of the people of the soil. Suddenly, those who worked the land appeared as "hayseeds" and "hicks" in vaudeville skits and comic strips.

But for the farmers and their families there were important things to worry about than the disdain of city folk. They faced a crippled economy, increasing competition, and the deterioration of the land itself. Even the future of their farms—maintained in many cases for generations—seemed in doubt as their sons and daughters left home for new lives in the nation's cities.

Historically, those engaged in agriculture traded the unending labor of farm work for a satisfyingly independent way of life. But in the 1890s, it seemed that the more agricultural products that the farmers produced, the less money they made. Railroad shipping rates ate up their profits, and the new farm implements necessary to increase efficiency threatened to put them deep into debt. Unhappy with their situation on the consuming end of life, many farmers joined the Grange, a cooperative purchasing group designed, in the words of the organization's motto, "to save the farmer's money by eliminating the middleman."

But things were not all bad for the farmer. The price of modern implements was high but they made work easier. Corn threshers, giant combines, and cream separators were just a few of the devices that gave a bit of leisure time to the 1890s tillers of the soil. Moreover, the upturn in the agricultural economy late in the decade provided some encouragement, while the spread of the railroad and the beginning of free rural mail delivery in 1896 helped ease the farmer's terrible isolation. Nonetheless, it was obvious to many that life on the farm was not what it used to be. The farmer's most treasured asset, his independence, was disappearing as railroads, equipment suppliers, and banks assumed control of his existence. What was once the most desirable way of life in America became known by a negative term: the farm problem.

George O. Boyce, a farmer in Montpelier, Vermont, sharpens a hay cutter blade while Sampson, his hired hand, turns the handle on the grindstone. Boyce's grandson closely observes the task, perhaps imagining himself in his grandfather's shoes one day.

(LEFT) *A farmer and a milkmaid enjoy a momentary respite during the long work day.*

(BELOW) *During most of the 19th century, large, extended families joined together to till the land. Here a lively group of men and women share the warmth of companionship while they work.*

(FOLLOWING PAGES) *Toward the end of the 19th century, the harvesting process was aided by a host of innovations, like this steam thresher, circa 1895.*

 A group of cyclists takes a break down by the riverside in Fenton, Missouri, in 1897.

The members of the Seventy Club of St. Johnsbury, Vermont, were dressed to the nines in 1899. Clubs and associations of all kinds were formed during the 1890s.

(OPPOSITE) *It was a time of fervent patriotism. Even the smallest citizen knew how to celebrate the Fourth of July.*

(LEFT) *Shooting marbles was a favorite pastime among boys of all ages.*

(BELOW) *What small town would have been complete without a swimming hole? Here, ladies and gents dressed in the modest swim attire of the day cool themselves at De Leon Springs in Florida.*

Richard W. Sears.   The 1894 edition of the Sears, Roebuck catalog.   Alvah C. Roebuck.

The Wish Book

Richard Sears knew a potential customer when he saw one—and in the 1890s, the small towns and farms of America were full of potential customers. A moderately priced mail-order business was just what rural folk needed, thought the young salesman, to ease the burden of high-priced goods offered by general stores and peddlers.

Combining his instincts for a lucrative business opportunity with old-fashioned common sense, Sears developed just such a catalog, one that became a dear friend to the isolated people of rural America. Boys dreamed over the picture of their first bicycle, while farmers and farmers' wives studied the corn shuckers and clothes and patent medicines.

The 23-year-old Sears had begun selling timepieces in 1886 before teaming up with a watch repairman named Alvah Roebuck. In 1891, the two entrepreneurs offered a watch catalog. Two years later, they expanded their offerings to 322 pages and included sewing machines, bicycles, pianos, and men's and boys' clothing. In 1894, the book also featured women's clothing, wagons, stoves, fishing tackle, seeds, and reading material. Other companies like Montgomery Ward produced catalogs too, but none became as popular as that of Sears, Roebuck.

One reason for the success of this "wish book" was that Sears knew how to communicate with farmers in a way that both entertained and reassured. On the front page of the catalog, he told them in his simple, folksy manner, "Don't be afraid that you will make a mistake. Tell us what you want in your own way, written in any language, no matter whether good or poor writing, and the goods will promptly be sent to you." He also kept ahead of his competitors by strict adherence to a "satisfaction guaranteed" policy and the use of printed testimonials and references throughout the catalog.

The visionary Sears wasn't as adept at managing the day-to-day operations of his enterprise, and as a result, the business was chaotic and operated at a frantic pace. In 1895, Roebuck decided the stress was too much and opted to sell out to his energetic partner for $25,000. However, he continued to work for Sears, who in the meantime formed a successful partnership with Aaron Nusbaum and Julius Rosenwald. In 1897, the company proudly distributed 318,000 catalogs—never dreaming that someday the wish book would go to 15 million homes.

 (LEFT) *An elaborately-decorated carriage stands ready to carry its eager passengers to a Mardi Gras celebration in Little Rock, Arkansas.*

 (BELOW) *It was a big event when the circus came to town. To announce their arrival—and to drum up business— troupers typically paraded down Main Street while the townfolk gawked and cheered.*

THE HUDDLED
MASSES

The Huddled Masses

During the 1890s, America was in the midst of the largest migration in the world's history, as more than 23.5 million people took up residence in the "land of opportunity" between 1880 and 1920. With this enormous flood of immigrants came a host of problems—unfair hiring practices and the lowering of wages, overcrowded housing, and the attendant increases in infectious diseases and crime rates. These ills helped harden the nation's attitudes toward immigrants. But still they came, those intrepid seekers that poet Emma Lazarus called the "tired," the "poor," the "huddled masses yearning to breathe free."

The immigrants of the 1890s were a different breed than their predecessors of the 1870s and 1880s. Whereas the latter were predominantly English, Irish, Scotch, and German, the newcomers came primarily from Eastern Europe, Russia, and Italy, and they were more heavily Catholic and Jewish. The former immigrants, many having the advantage of the same tongue and some of the same customs as their adopted country, merged with the American scene more easily than did the latter-day arrivals.

Nevertheless, the lure of America was much the same for the 1890s immigrants as it had been for those who had preceded them; it offered opportunities for education, jobs, religious freedom, and political choice the likes of which were unheard of in their homelands. In some

The dreaded exam at Ellis Island

East Side Peddlers, New York.

regions, emigration to America was even more than an opportunity—it was a lifesaver. Persecution of the Jews was reaching horrifying proportions in Russia, as massacres, or pogroms, wiped out whole villages. Finns, Lithuanians, and other ethnic groups suffering under the Russian Tsar sought to avoid compulsory military service and the Russian occupation of their countries. In order to escape desperate poverty, resulting from an exploding population and worn-out land, an estimated half a million Italians migrated to the United States in the 1890s. The exodus was so great that at the turn of the century, when one Italian mayor reportedly greeted a visitor, he did so on behalf of his constituents, "three thousand of whom are in America and the other five thousand [who are] preparing to follow them."

Even though the trip from Europe was long and arduous by today's standards, trains and steamships were making the trek easier. Just as the railroad had opened up the American frontier, so too did train transport in southern and eastern Europe, and Russia. In the outlying areas of these nations, residents were able to reach seaports with relative ease for the first time. Steamship companies actively recruited passengers, and although the fare often took the better part of a family's resources, most people could scrape up the funds for steerage at least. By 1894, new steamships boasting speeds of up to 24 knots and space for as many as 3,000 passengers offered passage for as low as $12.

(PREVIOUS PAGES) *Immigrants try to stay warm on the deck of the Red Star Line's SS* Westernland, *circa 1890.*

Some immigrants received tickets from relatives who had already emigrated. "Chain migration" they called it. Not only did the newcomers in America send passage or money to those in the old country, they sent information and encouragement as well. They also formed clubs and associations in America and these organizations helped ease the transition for new arrivals.

What was it like for immigrants and their children in the new land? For some it indeed became a chance for tremendous opportunity. A few like Samuel Goldwyn, Irving Berlin, and Helena Rubenstein found wealth and fame beyond their wildest expectations. But for many who thought the streets of the New World were literally paved with gold, the reality of life in America was intimidating, even overwhelming. Those who found the language, the customs, and the way of life alien and discomforting huddled together in enclaves where they could share the familiarity of the old ways. Thus Little Italies, Little Polands and Chinatowns were born.

Although many of those who immigrated to America in the 1890s came from rural environments back home, few of them sought to move inland and return to agricultural pursuits in the New World. Which was fortunate because there was little unclaimed arable land left in the United States. The South attracted few immigrants during this period, due in part to the lack of industrial jobs and in part to the anti-Catholic and anti-Semitic attitudes that were prevalent below the Mason-Dixon line. Thus most of the newcomers to America elected to live in the emerging metropolises of the Northeast and Midwest. They crammed into the dismal slums of New York's Lower East Side, huddled in the midst of the docks and markets of the North End of Boston, and packed into tenements near Chicago's slaughterhouses. As the decade progressed and thousands more arrived, housing shortages in these

Russians, Austrians, and other newcomers to America attend an English class in New York City.

One of the 1890s immigrants who "made it" in America was Irving Berlin (born Israel Baline), seen here in his 1943 hit This is the Army.

cities became critical, and many immigrants were forced to subsist in basements, former outhouses, or hastily constructed shacks behind tenements.

The new immigrants—mostly young males—filled the lowest stratum on the socioeconomic ladder. They took the least desirable jobs in the garment factories of New York, the coal mines and steel mills of Pennsylvania, and the slaughterhouses of Chicago. The influx of cheap, unskilled labor enabled employers to shut out the skilled laborers, and to ignore protests about low pay and poor working conditions. After all, they reasoned, they could always hire more workers "just off the boat."

Resentment and prejudice toward the immigrants became pronounced in the 1890s. Many native-born Americans began to look upon the newcomers, especially those from Eastern or Southern Europe, as racially inferior, dirty, and criminal. The Italians in particular were subject to hostility. Because many of them came to America as migratory workers, laboring for a season or a year, then returning to Italy, they were perceived as undesirable transients who weren't going to settle down and contribute to the nation's future.

In the years to come, the anti-immigrant feelings would lead to the end of America's open door policy. Thereafter quotas would be set to limit the numbers of foreigners who could settle in the United States. For the immigrants in the 1890s, however, America was still the promised land. When the steamships entered New York's harbor and the newcomers saw the Statue of Liberty, erected in 1886, they wept with joy. And they took the memory of that great lady with them out into the strange, new land, where they were determined to make successes of their new lives.

The solemn faces on these women reflect the uncertainty that many immigrants felt at leaving their homes and, in some cases, their families to seek new opportunities in America.

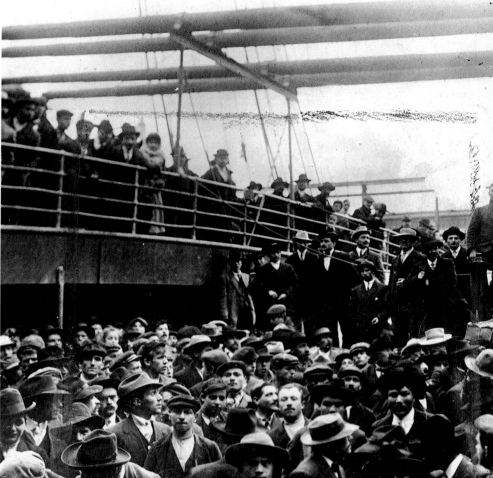

Newcomers from Italy cluster near the ship's rail in New York harbor to get a glimpse of their new homeland.

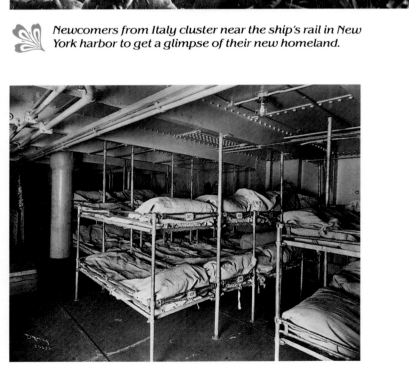

Sleeping accommodations in steerage were basic and very crowded.

The native dress of these Slavic immigrants was part of the colorful scene at Ellis Island in 1899.

(OPPOSITE) Families often had to come to America in increments, so many children like these were forced to make the trans-Atlantic journey by themselves.

The new federal facility for precessing immigrants opened on Ellis Island in 1892. It burned down five years later.

The Golden Door

It was called Ellis Island, a tiny land mass between New Jersey and New York that was little more than a sand bar. Here in 1892 the first immigration station operated by the United States government began processing prospective citizens. The reception hall wasn't quite ready for the first arrivals, but when it was finished, the vast room, with its 58-foot-high ceiling, could hold thousands of people waiting for clearance.

The process facing immigrants who wished to enter the United States was intimidating indeed. First, they were marched in long lines past doctors watching for handicaps or disease. Then they were given more specific exams, like the painful test for trachoma in which the eyelids were turned inside out. Finally, they were questioned about their background, destination, and financial status. The exams and interrogations were part of the new federal effort to shut out "undesirables," but newcomers to America in the 1890s were so happy to be in the promised land at last that nothing could dampen their enthusiasm.

Federal involvement in the processing of immigrants was new. Until the 1870s, control of those entering the country had been in the hands of the states, but over the years, a series of laws had gradually placed the responsibility within the purview of the federal government. In 1891, Congress gave the new U.S. Immigrant Bureau exclusive control over newcomers to America, and the new immigration station at Ellis Island opened officially the next year. Although a few immigrants entered through other cities, New York was the principal port of arrival.

Between 1892 and 1897, the complex at Ellis Island sometimes processed as many as 10,000 immigrants a day. It wasn't all onerous. Newcomers could change their money there and buy railroad tickets. And there were food stands and a dormitory for those detained overnight. In 1897, the complex was destroyed by a roaring blaze that consumed the wooden buildings but took no lives. The government rebuilt the complex with fireproof structures, and the new Ellis Island facility opened in 1900.

(LEFT) *Each step of the examination took time.*

(OPPOSITE TOP) *In addition to the processing facilities, Ellis Island offered immigrants some welcome services, including a place to exchange currency.*

(OPPOSITE BOTTOM) *Many were surprised by the unfamiliar food served at Ellis Island.*

 (OPPOSITE) *Immigrants like these Italians—photographed in Chicago by Lewis Hine—endured appalling living conditions in the hope of making a better life for their children.*

(LEFT) *Although overcrowding exacerbated problems like juvenile delinquency, alcoholism, and violence, most immigrants struggled to make good homes in their adopted country.*

(BELOW) *Most immigrant families took in boarders, turning many three-room apartments, like the one shown here, into homes for fourteen people.*

The vast majority of Europeans immigrating to America in the 1890s came through Ellis Island in New York harbor. Some moved on to other cities but millions stayed to make New York their home . . .

 (ABOVE) *Jewish immigrants, principally from Russia, created an enclave for themselves on Manhattan's Lower East Side.*

(RIGHT) *Fresh flowers were a luxury that few immigrants could afford to buy but they offered a commodity that women could sell to others.*

(LEFT) *In this typical East Side market, pushcart peddlers sold just about everything necessary for survival in the tenements.*

(BELOW) *On wash day, every inch of space outside the tenements was occupied.*

Faced with strange new customs and, in many cases, an unfamiliar language, newcomers frequently banded together to share common interests and to preserve familiar ways of life . . .

 A Chinese shopkeeper in San Francisco's Chinatown.

(OPPOSITE) Recreational and athletic activities for young people were offered by German societies called Turnvereins in many American cities. Here a men's gymnastics team from the Turnverein in St. Louis, Missouri, performs on the horizontal bars (opposite top) and the women engage in a bar drill (opposite below).

 (ABOVE) *The weather-beaten face of this Polish woman is a testament to the years of struggle and determination endured by millions of 19th-century immigrants.*

 (LEFT) *Children play in front of a Polish saloon in Chicago around the turn of the century. The Windy City has the second largest Polish community in the world (Warsaw, of course, has the first).*

This Hispanic family poses outside of its home in Trinidad, Colorado; the family patriarch is seated before the doorway of the adobe dwelling. Numerous Hispanic communities were established in the Southwest long before the Anglo settlements that grew up around them.

Arts and Entertainment

Buffalo Bill Cody, former Indian fighter and adventurer turned showman.

There was no radio, of course. Or television. Or movies, although Edison's invention of the motion picture would constitute one of the marvels of the decade. There were phonograph records—and they represented a significant first step in the coming democratization of entertainment. But for the most part, those seeking drama or dance or music in the 1890s gathered, as people had for centuries, to see live entertainers in performance.

Perhaps no one epitomized the world of show business in the 1890s better than William Frederick Cody. He was rough, self-confident, and full of the entrepeneurial spirit—like America itself. A former army scout and buffalo hunter who earned the nickname "Buffalo Bill" for his prodigious ability to slaughter the wooly beasts, Cody formed his "Wild West Show and Congress of Rough Riders of the World" in 1883. He organized cowboys and Indians and other frontier characters into an entertainment that was part circus, part vaudeville, and part something completely original. Mixing marksmanship exhibitions featuring the likes of sureshot Annie Oakley with horse races and "spectaculars" like the attack on the

Deadwood stage, he brought a romanticized view of the Wild West to the folks back East and, later to the folks in Europe—and folks everywhere loved it. In 1893, the show came to Chicago where it parked outside the World's Columbian Exposition, the Windy City's spectacular fair commemorating Columbus's voyage to the New World, and in one year, Cody earned a whopping $1 million profit.

Meanwhile, inside the fair's utopian White City, ladies swooned over the passionate sonatas of classical pianist Paderewski and everybody tapped their toes to the syncopated rhythms of African-American composer Scott Joplin. Joplin's music, known as ragtime, would later develop into that distinctively American art form, jazz.

For those who liked their entertainment fast and breezy there was also vaudeville. With its roots in the medicine show and minstrel show and the saloon-like variety halls called honky-tonks that flourished in the 1880s, vaudeville offered an incredibly diversified bill of fare—singers, comedians, dance teams, jugglers, magicians, kiddie acts, animal acts, and novelties. Even Helen Keller, assisted by Anne Sullivan, "played" vaudeville. In its heyday, the popular form of entertainment boasted great circuits of theaters established by the likes of Alexander Pantages, Benjamin Franklin Keith, and Klaw and Erlanger. But for the elite, the place to play in the 1890s

The inventor of ragtime, Scott Joplin.

(PREVIOUS PAGES) *This elaborately-decorated theater in Salt Lake City, Utah, featured a curtain painting by Alfred Cambowen.*

The glamorous music hall star, Lillian Russell.

was the Fourteenth Street Theater in New York City owned by the dapper Tony Pastor. Harrigan and Hart, Weber and Fields, Buster Keaton, the Four Cohans—these were among the headliners at Pastor's theater. But Tony's favorite was none other than Lillian Russell.

Born in 1861 as Helen Louise Leonard, Lillian Russell made her debut in the chorus of Gilbert and Sullivan's *H.M.S. Pinafore* in 1879 and two year's later starred in *Grand Mogul* by Edmond Audran. But it was as a featured attraction at Pastor's theater that she gained widespread fame. With her striking good looks and voluptuous figure, she came to embody the era's ideal of feminine beauty and was perhaps the most photographed woman of her day. Even the judge in a legal dispute arising from her refusal to wear tights maintained that Lillian's figure was a national asset.

The 1890s also saw the continuing development of a realistic style in American literature. *The Red Badge of Courage,* published in 1895, showcased the hard-edged brilliance of the young Stephen Crane, while the impact of Mark Twain's *Huckleberry Finn* (1885) continued to reverberate. Writers who would emerge after the turn of the century, like poet Carl Sandburg and novelist Edith Wharton, were already chronicling the life and times of Chicagoans and New Yorkers, respectively.

In Europe, the 1890s saw new modes of expression find their way into the fine and decorative arts, as well as classical music and literature. Art nouveau, a richly ornamental style with curvilinear shapes and asymmetrical compositions, swept the continent. Known by a variety of names including Jugendstil in Germany, Secessionism in Austria, and Modernismo in Spain, it was manifest in the highly decorative paintings of Vienna's Gustav Klimt, the impossibly curvacious architecture of Barcelona's Antoni Gaudí, the sleek pen-and-ink graphics of London's Aubrey Beardsley, and the brilliantly colored lamps of New York's Louis Comfort Tiffany. Drama took a sharp turn in the direction of realism through the plays of Norway's Henrik Ibsen, whose *Hedda Gabler* premiered in 1891 and Russia's Anton Chekhov, whose *Uncle Vanya* debuted six years later. Inspired by the works of Ibsen, George Bernard Shaw delivered social criticism in the guise of sardonic wit with such early works as *Arms and the Man* and *Candida,* both of which premiered in London in the 1890s. Shaw's fellow utopian socialist, H. G. Wells,

believed the world could be improved through science and was thus inspired to write his imaginative fantasies, *The Time Machine* in 1895 and *War of the Worlds* in 1898. And Sir Arthur Conan Doyle introduced scientific criminology—including fingerprinting—into his enormously popular Sherlock Holmes stories that ran in *Strand* Magazine beginning in 1891. Finally Oscar Wilde concocted wry sophisticated comedies of upper-class life in plays like *Lady Windermere's Fan* (1892) and *The Importance of Being Earnest.* He also produced his gothic horror novel, *The Picture of Dorian Gray* in 1891, and a scandalous look at the Bible, *Salome,* in 1893. Imprisoned for sodomy in 1895, Wilde served two years in Reading Gaol and died soon after his release, at the age of 46.

Europe also saw an explosion of composition in classical music and opera, as French composers Claude Debussy, and Maurice Ravel made waves with early works, while Giacomo Puccini's career took off with the 1896 premiere of *La Bohème,* one of the most popular operas of all time. The 1890s also saw the unhappy dissolution of the partnership of Gilbert and Sullivan, the brilliant British team that had enlivened the world with comic operas like *The Mikado* in the previous decade.

Many of Europe's innovations found their way to the United Sates in the 1890s as artists from abroad began to seriously tap the large and relatively entertainment hungry audiences in America. Among them was Peter Ilyich Tchaikovsky, who created *Swan Lake* and *The Nutcracker Suite* in the 1890s. The world famous Russian composer participated in the opening of New York's Carnegie Hall in 1891. Two years later, Antonin Dvořák, the popular Czech composer, premiered his *New World Symphony* there.

In the long run, however, the most memorable performance of the decade may have come when Lillian Russell sang *The Sabre Song* into a large metal funnel in her dressing room at New York's Casino Theater in 1890. A special telephone line connected her to President Benjamin Harrison in Washington D. C. It was the opening of the first long-distance telephone line, and although the impact of this event extended far beyond show business, it symbolized a new link in the relationship between entertainment and technology. In the decades to come, that link would become a revolution that would transform the world.

Czech composer, Antonin Dvořák.

73

Thomas Alva Edison (1847—1931), circa 1890.

The Kinetoscope and Mr. Edison

O ne dropped a coin in the slot and peered into a peephole. A mysterious, two-inch-high man appeared—and sneezed. It doesn't sound like much, but in 1894, it was the first time most Americans had seen a picture that moved. And so they thronged to Thomas A. Edison's kinetoscope parlors to see the ordinary on film—a horse eating hay, a girl dancing, and two men boxing.

The kinetoscope was a cabinet with 50 feet of celluloid film inside revolving on spools. To Edison it was a novelty item and, caught up in lab experiments on other projects, he failed to recognize the public's growing interest in his invention. To save money, he even let some of the patents slip away, allowing other inventors to develop their versions of the peephole machine in the United States and Europe. When Edison finally awoke to the potential monetary rewards from moving pictures, he began to manufacture more and bigger models of his kinetoscope, cranking up the price as he went. But he failed to recognize another development: the projection of moving pictures onto a screen where a room full of people could watch them at the same time. In only a year, the public was yawning over kinetoscopes, but the taste for the "flickers" was hardly whetted. About that time, a real estate man named Thomas Arnat came out of nowhere with the Vitascope, the best-designed projector so far. A large amount of cash and pressure from the world-famous Edison induced Arnat to give up credit for his invention.

Edison became even more famous for "his" latest marvel and the public fell in love with the big screen—especially with the release of a daring film showing a couple smooching. Thus a new American industry and a new art form were born. And with them came the first cries of protest and outrage—a hint of the many to follow over the immorality of both.

74

 (OPPOSITE) *Fred Ott's sneeze is reportedly the first close-up ever filmed.*

 (BELOW) *Edison created his first motion pictures in this ramshackle 1893 addition to his laboratory in West Orange, New Jersey. Called the Black Maria, it was the world's first movie studio.*

(BOTTOM) *This kinetoscope parlor offered peep shows, including one of heavyweight boxing champ, James J. Corbett. Patrons could also try another of Edison's celebrated inventions, the phonograph.*

 Russian composer Peter Ilyich Tchaikovsky visited the U.S. and presided over the opening of Carnegie Hall just two years before his death in 1893. Two of his most notable compositions, Sleeping Beauty *and* The Nutcracker, *were created in the 1890s.*

 (OPPOSITE) *Italian composer Giacomo Puccini, seen here with his librettist Illica, wrote his famous opera* La Bohême *in 1896.*

By the 1890s, a "refined" vaudeville had replaced the rough burlesque shows that had catered to working-class males . . .

 (LEFT) *In addition to comedy, vaudevillians performed acrobatics, songs, and short dramas, succeeding one another at a breakneck pace.*

 (BELOW) *Comedy teams like the one pictured here were among the mainstays of vaudeville. Typically these acts featured old-fashioned "low comedy" with plenty of pratfalls and fake fisticuffs.*

 (OPPOSITE) *Kiddie performers were among the most popular of the novelty acts to fill the bill in vaudeville during the 1890s.*

Letter to the World

Emily Dickinson's family had been unaware that during the last 25 years of her life, the shy spinster had written nearly 1,800 poems. When they discovered this treasure trove following her death in 1886, they wanted the work published for their own private delectation—they certainly didn't expect anybody else to want to read her poems. Some family members thought the work was so "crude" that it shouldn't be published at all. In 1891, Roberts Brothers was persuaded to publish a small edition, simply entitled *Poems*. To everyone's amazement, it sold out immediately. Ten more editions followed over the next two years, a new book appeared in 1891, and the *Letters of Emily Dickinson* followed in 1894.

Dickinson was born in 1830 in Amherst, Massachusetts. She seldom left the area, spending the last 25 years of her life in almost total seclusion and communicating with most friends through letters. She had a horror of being published, although one poem did appear in an anthology while she was alive. The poems of the reclusive genius might have disappeared forever, had it not been for Mabel Todd, a close friend of the family. She took on the enormous job of sorting and editing the myriad works written on scraps of paper in Emily's hard-to-read script.

Todd's most difficult work lay in convincing the literary world that Dickinson's strange form of writing was true poetry. She finally awakened one editor to their beauty by reading the poems aloud. After the work was published, however, her imagery was hailed by critics and public alike and the fascination with Dickinson and her poetry has continued until today. Despite the outpouring of words from her pen, the life of Emily Dickinson remained an enigma, living up to her lines: "Tell all the Truth but tell it slant/ Success in Circuit lies."

(LEFT) *In the early 1890s, the astonishing poems of Emily Dickinson were published—and acclaimed as works of genius.*

(OPPOSITE) *Born in 1873, to an alcoholic father and an invalid mother and raised in the crowded slums of Naples, the brilliant tenor Enrico Caruso made his first operatic appearance in 1895 at the Teatro Nuovo in his hometown. Here he is seen, striking a dramatic pose in his most famous role, Canio, in* Il Pagliaci.

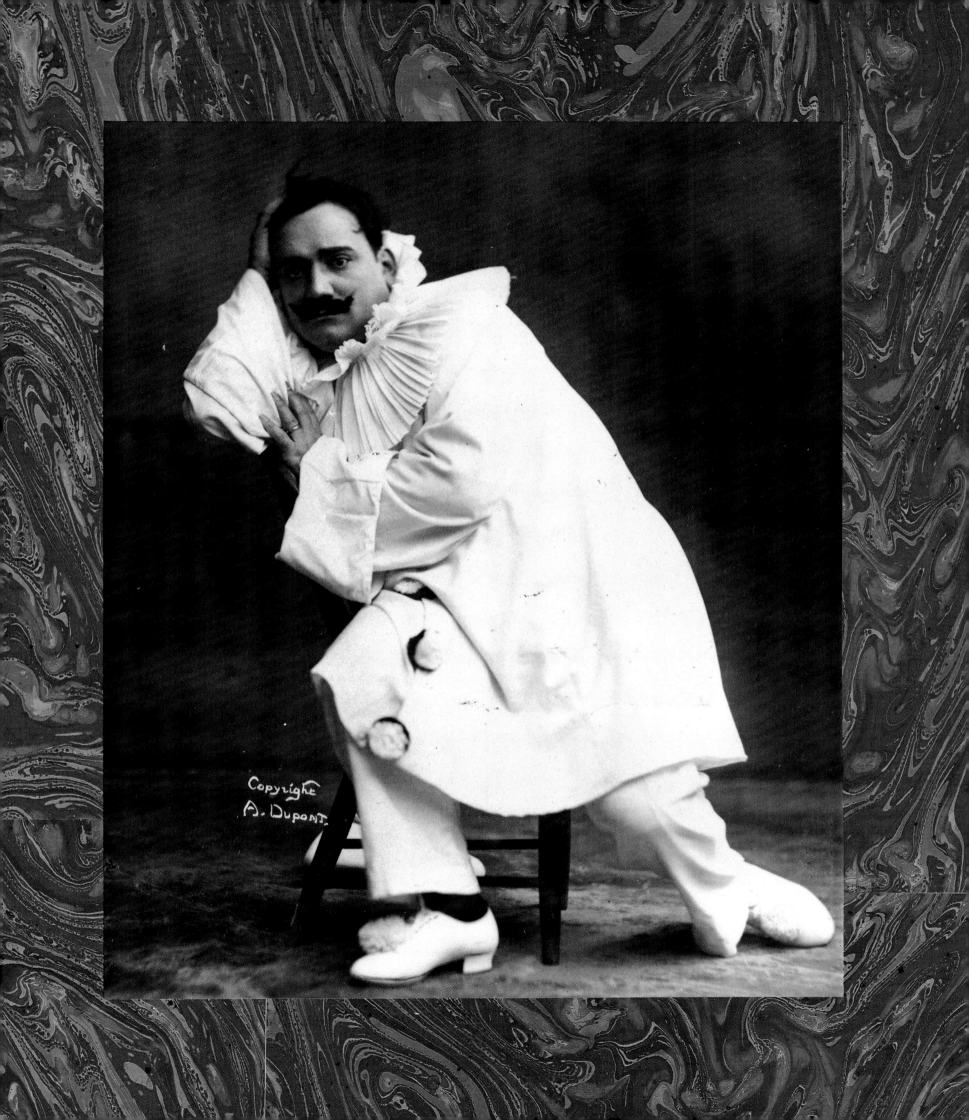

A Gift to the People of France

With his death in 1894, the Impressionist painter Gustave Caillebotte sparked a controversy that reached the highest circles of France. The subject was art. To be specific, the art of Caillebotte's contemporaries, those radicals Edgar Degas, Claude Monet, Pierre Auguste Renoir, Camille Pissaro, and Paul Cézanne.

Unlike most of his friends, Caillebotte was born to wealth. When his father died in 1874, he inherited a successful textile business and the freedom to pursue his interest in art. He also collected the works of the painters with whom he exhibited, in part because he could afford to help them out and in part because he genuinely admired their talents. No doubt, Monet, Renoir, Cézanne, and Pissaro welcomed Gustave's support, because their work had been denigrated by academicians, critics, and the public alike since their initial exhibition in 1874. Even the term "Impressionism" was derisive, bestowed upon the loosely organized group as a means of separating their works—full of dabs of color and quick brush strokes—from the tightly controlled renderings that were exhibited at the prestigious Salons.

In 1894, at the age of 45, Caillebotte died. But he left behind an impressive collection of 65 works by his peers, works that he donated to France in the hope that their display in the Louvre would bestow legitimacy upon the modern French school. The only problem was that the French government didn't want them. "Why did your friend decide to send us this white elephant?" one official asked Renoir, the executor of Caillebotte's estate.

For three years, the controversy over Caillebotte's bequest raged in the corridors of the Ministry of Fine Arts and in the press. Finally, in 1897, a compromise was reached. Much of the collection was refused—a great many of these paintings ended up in the United States—but 38 works were accepted, to be stored at the Luxembourg Museum, however, not the Louvre.

In the end, of course, Caillebotte triumphed. Although the painters of the French Academy have largely been forgotten, the works that he collected, including *The Balcony* by Edouard Manet, *The Train Station at Saint-Lazare* by Claude Monet, *The Star* by Edgar Degas, and *Dancing at the Moulin de la Galette* by Auguste Renoir, form the core of the Impressionist collection at the Musée D'Orsay in Paris, where they are among the most beloved paintings in the history of art.

 La Moulin de la Galette *by Pierre Auguste Renoir, the executor of Caillebotte's estate. This masterpiece was part of the Caillebotte bequest in 1894.*

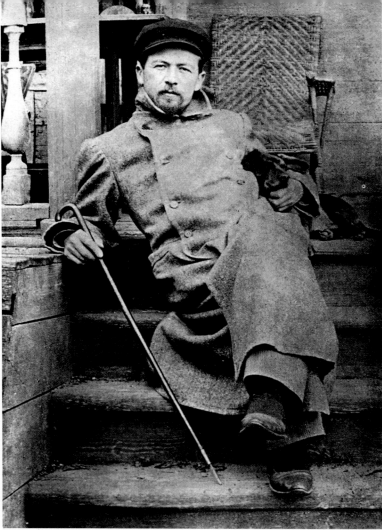

The European and American writers of the 1890s brought forth unique styles and new ideas. The works that they created would have a significant impact on the literature and plays of the 20th century . . .

This page

 (TOP LEFT) *Oscar Wilde, Irish poet, dramatist and the master of scintilating, witty dialogue.*

(RIGHT) *Mark Twain, America's most famous author. He toured the world as a lecturer during the 1890s.*

(BOTTOM LEFT) *Norwegian playwright Henrik Ibsen, who helped introduce realism in drama.*

Opposite page

 (TOP LEFT) *The youthful Stephen Crane, a prolific novelist and short story writer until his death in 1900.*

(BOTTOM LEFT) *Sir Author Conan Doyle, creator of the Sherlock Holmes detective stories.*

(TOP RIGHT) *The Russian Anton Chekhov, who began writing his acclaimed short stories in the 1890s while still a practicing physician.*

 (BOTTOM RIGHT) *H. G. Wells, an English journalist and novelist, who published his first book,* The Time Machine, *in 1895.*

85

 (RIGHT) *Edwin Booth, recognized as America's first great tragic actor, made his final appearance on stage, as Hamlet, in 1891.*

 (BELOW) *Buffalo Bill Cody created a uniquely American phenomenon with his Wild West Show. It toured the U.S. and the world in the late 1800s.*

The Sousa Sound

When he came to town, it was a holiday. Businesses closed, schools were dismissed, and people from near and far hurried to the park or the concert hall to hear the man who had revolutionized American music.

In 1890, John Philip Sousa had already gained fame as the conductor of the Marine Band; in a 20-year affiliation, he had built the organization into the premier military band in the country. He was also a well-established composer, whose first big hit was *The Washington Post,* which premiered in 1889. It was adapted to a new dance called the two-step, which replaced the waltz and swept both Europe and America in the 1890s, as the Twist would do some 70 years later. Sousa became known everywhere as "The March King." But as long as his band was part of the military establishment, he was restricted as an entertainer. He certainly couldn't tour with the Marine Band very often. So when a powerful band promoter offered Sousa a big salary and the opportunity to form his own civilian concert band, he bade farewell to the Marines. This departure marked the beginning of 39 more years of success for the March King.

The first public concert by the new Sousa Band took place in 1892 in New Jersey. Thereafter John Philip and his band toured the United States to increasingly large crowds. In 1896, they expanded into Canada and later into Europe, where they significantly altered the continent's disdain for American musicians. The multitalented Sousa also won more fans at home with his operettas and waltzes. But the stirring marches that he created—and one in particular, *The Stars and Stripes Forever*—have ensured his immortality.

Sousa's band eventually made four world tours and its leader became a millionaire, but it was in the 1890s that John Philip Sousa became an American institution. His fervent patriotism and the snappy rhythms that he extolled were in perfect harmony with the spirit of the age.

"The March King," John Philip Sousa.

A Birthday Party for Columbus

In the Chicago of 1893, the height of culture and civilization mixed freely with popular entertainment and downright vulgarity, as the Windy City celebrated the 400th anniversary of Christopher Columbus's discovery of America. Formally called the World's Columbian Exposition, the fair offered technological achievements and works of art in grand halls filled with 65,000 different exhibitions. People were awed by the accomplishments on display, but the single biggest draw in the huge fair was designed solely for fun. It was called the Ferris wheel.

This was the world's first such thrill ride, and it was a gem. At 264 feet, it provided a sweeping view of the enormous fair in Jackson Park. Fully loaded, it carried 2,160 people. Its large cars were the size of railroad coaches. The Ferris wheel was located in the Midway Plaisance, a mile-long stretch of noise and confusion filled with restaurants, shops, and a mind-boggling array of human and animal entertainment.

The Midway was the place one went after tiring of the high-minded Court of Honor. Spectators crowded together to watch lions riding horses in Hagenbeck's Animal Show and to ogle Little Egypt as she performed the hootchy-kootchy dance. To the dismay of many, the "dirty and barbaric" Midway became the most popular area of the fair. Indeed, the word thereafter became a generic term for an amusement park's main street.

During the six-month fair, there were 27,529,400 admissions. The visitors tramped through a model experimental farm, passing an 11-ton cheese and countless other pavilions in the monumental Hall of Agriculture. If one had the energy, one could also visit each state's separate building, tour Machinery Hall, and take a look at the 74 galleries of sculpture and paintings from the United States and Europe. A team of architects, Smithsonian scholars, and designers like Frederick Law Olmsted received high praise for the elegant and antiseptic White City that quietly surrounded the earthy Midway. The magnificent buildings, waterways, and grounds, built on what had been a swamp, seemed to symbolize the triumph of American know-how in uncertain times. One thing was for sure, however. Whether one went for the culture, the last word in gadgetry, or just plain fun, the World's Columbian Exposition was the highlight of the age and no one who saw it forgot it.

(OPPOSITE) *The Chicago Exposition brought a glimpse of other cultures to Americans, with elaborate exhibits, foreign foods, and even camel rides.*

(LEFT) *The immensity of the world's first Ferris wheel dominated the midway.*

(BELOW) *The grandeur of the White City helped change the image of the U.S. abroad, and significantly influenced American architecture in the years that followed.*

THE CLOSING OF THE FRONTIER

The Closing of The Frontier

During the 1890s, the onrush of civilization was rapidly changing the face of the western United States. Farms were claiming the open range. The Indian Wars were coming to an end and Native Americans were being pushed further and further into enclaves called reservations. And towns were becoming cities, with many of the amenities of city life—theaters, mass transit, law and order. Gone were the lively, but dangerous shoot-'em-up days of old. Still, a few trappings of frontier life could be found making their last stand against the onrush of change. Cowboys continued to herd cattle to the railheads throughout the decade, and outlaws, such as the Dalton Gang and the Wild Bunch, still earned their living in the old-fashioned way. But the impact of civilization was such that, in 1893, historian Frederick Jackson Turner declared the American frontier closed.

Perhaps the biggest single factor in the metamorphosis of the West was the coming of the railroad. President Abraham Lincoln had once predicted that it would take at least a century to settle the rugged frontier lands, but he had not counted on the power of the steam locomotive. The United States had about 35,000 miles of track at the time of Lincoln's assassination; by 1890, that total had risen to more than 164,000 miles. When trains rolled down those tracks, they brought hundreds of thousands of land-hungry people with them. They also brought badly needed supplies and provided the Western entrepreneur with a conduit to the major markets in the East. Railroad companies were not oblivious to their pivotal role in Western commerce, however. They kept raising freight tariffs until many frontier businessmen and farmers were ruined.

By 1890, there were more than 164,000 miles of railroad track in the U.S.

Big Foot, the respected leader of the Miniconjou Sioux, perished at the Battle of Wounded Knee.

If the avalanche of people coming West gave life to the region in the form of new towns and farms, it also spelled trouble for the great cattle empires. The herds that once roamed a vast open range stretching from the Missouri River to the Rocky Mountains found themselves confined to smaller and smaller grazing areas as settlers and the U.S. government carved up the land. The ranchers themselves made matters worse by overgrazing the range; the terrible blizzards of 1885/86 and 1886/87 contributed to the decline of the herds as well.

Beyond the railroad, the West was experiencing an explosion of technology in the 1890s. The telegraph, facilitated rapid communication with the rest of the nation. And advances like the steel plow, barbed wire, and the windmill made it possible for settlers to break the sod and raise crops in areas previously considered to be too arid for farming. Still there were more farmers than there was arable land. Soon white settlers were clamoring for the federal government to open up the 14 million acres known as the Indian Territory, or Oklahoma. When the government finally acquiesced, Oklahoma became the site of the most dramatic and accelerated pattern of settlement in the history of the West.

The first great land run occurred in 1889, after the U.S.

(PREVIOUS PAGES) *Determined homesteaders built shake cabins and tilled the soil in the timbered wilderness of Washington.*

Sightseers enjoy the breath-taking view of America's first national park, Yosemite, created in 1890.

government had acquired 2 million acres in the heart of the Indian Territory from the Seminoles and Creeks. More runs took place as other Oklahoma tribes were forced to accept payments for their lands. The most infamous came with the opening of the Cherokee Outlet in 1893. More than 100,000 people stampeded into the fertile 58-by-100 mile strip along the Kansas border on a hot day in September. Desperation and confusion were heightened by the 100 degree temperature and the knowledge that there was little good land left in the West. Some people were willing to do anything to get a stake. Soon after the run, the body of a man with his throat slit was found hidden in a hollow.

A diverse population settled the territory: Kansans, Texans, impoverished farmers from all the southern states, Mennonite farmers from Germany, Italian miners, and Jewish merchants from Austria and Bavaria. But, as different as they were, they shared a common determination to succeed. And despite the harshness and hardships of those first years, most did.

Another opportunity for success opened up in 1896 in an even more remote and inhospitable region—the far Northwest of Canada and Alaska. Before the 1890s, the rugged Yukon and Alaskan territories were unknown to all but a few hardy miners and the native "Esquimaux." But once the word gold was mentioned, the distance and the obstacles became unimportant: the Klondike rush of '98 was on. The gold—so much gold that a hard worker could pan $5,000 worth in just one day—brought in an estimated 100,000 fortune hunters. They arrived after difficult and dangerous journeys only to discover that every inch of ground had long since been claimed by those who had been there for a decade. Still they got to experience one of the great adventures of all time, an adventure that also included some of the worst living conditions on earth. In the boom towns of Dawson City and Grand Forks, for example, prices became so inflated that a gallon of whiskey cost $40. Temperatures reached 50 degrees below zero in the winter, and in the warmer months, the region played host to mosquitoes, mud, malaria, and the stench from the sewage and garbage. Most of the gold seekers of '96 ended up broke and disillusioned. While they headed back to milder climates, subsequent strikes brought new fortune seekers to

Nome, Fairbanks, and other sites. Although none were as dramatic as the frantic Klondike rush, the successive waves of miners and merchants carved a trail that opened up the Northwestern wilderness.

Meanwhile, as the new civilization was emerging across the West, an older one was virtually disappearing. It was becoming easier and easier to forget that another people once lived on this land. The Native Americans didn't farm it or put sheep on it or cut down the trees on it, and so the white settlers felt little sympathy for them or the end of their way of life. As for the Indians, they had struggled unsuccessfully for decades against the encroaching white pioneers and they had no fight left. Thus, in the 1890s, the Indian Wars came to an end. Many of the remaining Native Americans lived in abject poverty. Their children were taken far away to Indian schools, where they were dressed in white men's clothes, forbidden to speak their own "barbarous" dialects, and taught the white way of living. One school director summed up the educational philosophy with the sentiment, "Kill the Indian and save the man."

The shocking changes in the lives of the Indians extended to the very ground they walked on, because the environment itself was affected by the onslaught of "civilization." In Oklahoma, for example, the great grassy plains that had been rich in wild flowers and wild animals were transformed almost overnight. "The road and the plowing had changed the shape of the country," said a Kiowa, looking back on that time, "the feel of the world had changed." But on this issue—concern for the environment—Native Americans weren't alone. California became the first serious battleground between those who sought to protect the land and those who sought to develop it. Lumbermen, ranchers, and farmers were outraged at the suggestion that they should curtail their profit-making schemes in deference to the natural beauty around them. But a long campaign to preserve some of the most spectacular scenery in the West resulted in an important development in 1890, when Congress created national parks protecting Yosemite, Sequoia, and the grove of giant Sequoias called General Grant.

Farms, fences, and national parks—the signs of civilization were appearing in the most remote places. For better or worse, in the 1890s, the West stopped being wild.

Prospectors in Alaska in the 1890s.

(BELOW) *The intersection of Congress Avenue and 5th Street in downtown Austin, Texas.*

 (OPPOSITE TOP) *A prospector's burros wait patiently for their owner on San Francisco Street in Santa Fe, New Mexico.*

(OPPOSITE BOTTOM) *Denver, Colorado, was a well-established city by the end of the 19th century, with imposing hotels, churches and the clutter of telephone wires and trolley car lines framing Broadway.*

Cowboys

In the 1890s, cowboys were still cowboys. They still worked on horseback using the skills and equipment originally passed on to them by the Mexican vaquero. They still wore broad-brimmed hats, chaps, and bandanas. And they still roped, branded, and herded cattle. But they also had to mend barbed-wire fences, grease windmills, and do other alien tasks. The new jobs reflected the change from life on the open range to life on a ranch.

Previously, a cowhand's life had been noticeably lacking in boundaries. The roundups and long trail drives that took herds to the railheads occurred in wide, open spaces. The cowpuncher, as he called himself then, lived an independent, nomadic life. But it was as spartan an existence as a man could have. A cowpuncher owned a saddle, clothes, and bedding; he had few creature comforts. He worked long hours in desert heat and winter blizzards and was frequently injured, not so much by gunfire as by throws from his horse and hard knocks in cattle stampedes. His nearly nonexistent social life revolved around the chuck wagon and rare trips to town.

Texas was central to the cowboy culture, because it was in the Lone Star state that ranchers had started the system of trail drives that took cheaply grown cattle to Dodge City, Abilene, and other Midwestern destinations. The Texas cowboys who herded the cattle on these long treks were acclaimed for their exuberance and fearlessness, but angry farmers in their path viewed them in a more negative light. In the end, the farmers won, and by the turn of the century, the railroads had advanced into cattle country and the trail drives died out. Now confined to ranches, the cowboys had to learn to be neighborly with the "sodbusters," being unable to ride away into the sunset as they had in the past. Meanwhile, their numbers began to diminish with the diminution of the ranches themselves.

While cowpunchers began to sleep in bunkhouses and settle down along with the rest of the West during the 1890s, their style of dress, and their code of conduct—as stoics and rugged individualists—came to symbolize America. Even today, the mythic status of the American cowboy endures around the world.

(OPPOSITE) *A cowpuncher with all the essentials—a broad-brimmed hat to block the sun, a kerchief to protect his nose and mouth from dust, and chaps to shield his pants from high grass.*

(RIGHT) *A greenhorn feebly attempts to master a lariat, while the experienced hands look on with amusement.*

(BELOW) *A cattle roundup in western Oklahoma in the 1890s.*

 (OPPOSITE) *Photographer Charles L. Joy (kneeling) joined this pioneer family in a portrait centered around the sturdy wagon that brought them west.*

 (RIGHT) *This stereoptican slide offers a sentimental view of frontier family life, with the clan—three generations of them—gathered in front of their log cabin for some after-supper fiddle music.*

(BELOW) *The Barber family home in Oklahoma. Although they were unglamorous, sod dugouts offered pioneers a warm and secure haven.*

One of the surest signs that the frontier was coming to a close was the replacement of rule by gun with rule by law . . .

 (OPPOSITE TOP) *Judge Roy Bean was, in his own words, the "Law West of the Pecos." He may have dispensed rough justice, but most inhabitants in the sparsely settled West Texas were grateful for any kind of law enforcement.*

(OPPOSITE BOTTOM) *The remains of the notorious Dalton Gang following their foolhardy attempt to rob both banks in Coffeyville, Kansas, in 1892. Emmett Dalton was the only survivor of the Coffeyville raid.*

(BELOW) *The notorious Sugar House Prisoners in the Utah State Penitentiary. They were imprisoned for defying the laws against polygamy.*

 (ABOVE) *In the wake of the opening of the Indian Territory to white settlement, bustling towns sprang up nearly overnight. A case in point is Round Pond, with its grandly-named Broadway Street, seen here in 1894.*

(RIGHT) *The Cherokee Outlet land rush on September 16, 1893, was the most famous of the five runs in Oklahoma. Anyone wishing to claim a parcel of the former Indian lands could do so on a first-come, first-served basis.*

(OPPOSITE) *The Guthrie Cotton Market at the peak of trading, circa 1893. In one corner of this busy scene is another photographer setting up his camera.*

A Good Day to Die

By 1890, the buffalo were gone, and the great Indian leaders were dead or pacified. Reservation life was killing the spirit of the surviving Plains Indians. In desperation, the Sioux embraced a new religion, one that promised to bring back the buffalo and the old way of life. At the core of this new religion was the sacred ghost dance. As the dancing became more frequent, the officials at the Indian agencies in South Dakota grew uneasy. One army commander decided to arrest Chief Sitting Bull, the famed medicine man who was encouraging the ghost dancers. But when an army officer accompanied by Indian police entered Sitting Bull's cabin, a conflict erupted and the leader of the Sioux was shot to death in his own bed.

The news swept the countryside, causing panic. Chief Big Foot and his band of about 350 Sioux men, women, and children, already alarmed by the rumors of their relocation, feared that the killing of Sitting Bull signaled the start of a wholesale slaughter. So they fled north on a bitterly cold day in December 1890. Big Foot rode in the first wagon, ill and helpless and hoping that if he could not entirely evade the U.S. Army, he could at least avert disaster for his people. Then his scouts told him that a cavalry troop was approaching, and he decided to surrender.

The whites and the Indians camped together at Wounded Knee Creek, but the uneasy soldiers grew res-

tive when a shaman began the ghost dance. The Indians became equally alarmed when the soldiers started searching their lodges and under the skirts of the women for weapons. There was a scuffle, a gunshot, and then the killing began: the army opened fire with its repeating Hotchkiss cannons trained directly on the Sioux camp, killing approximately 300, including 62 women and children. Twenty-nine soldiers were also killed, some of them no doubt by friendly fire.

There was an outcry in the press about the slaughter of noncombatants, and the military conducted some inquiries. A few bands of outraged Sioux tried to retaliate for the massacre, but Wounded Knee fundamentally brought an end to the Indian Wars. For the Native American, it marked the bitter conclusion to a cherished way of life. As Oglala medicine man Black Elk said, "A people's dream died there."

(ABOVE) *The body of the Sioux leader Big Foot, frozen in the snow at Wounded Knee, South Dakota, where he was killed in the 1890 battle. (see p. 92 for a portrait of Big Foot)*

(OPPOSITE) *At the height of the Klondike Gold rush in 1898, an unending stream of would-be prospectors ascended the heights of the Chilkoot Pass.*

Three Western states entered the Union in the 1890s . . .

(LEFT) *Idaho became the 43rd state in 1890, just ahead of Wyoming. These citizens of Idaho City marked the occasion with appropriate attire.*

  (ABOVE) *A statehood parade in Cheyenne, Wyoming in 1890.*

(RIGHT) *Twelve-year-old Tilly Houtz was crowned Queen of Utah Statehood in 1896.*

The Last of the Legendary Outlaws

The sheriff's posse determinedly picked its way up the rugged trail to the rim of a steep cliff in a remote corner of northern Wyoming. When the lawmen had made their way through the notch at the top, they reined up and scratched their heads. They may have been able to track Butch Cassidy and his gang to the "Hole-in-the-Wall," but after looking around, they knew they'd never find them within that secluded valley. It was full of little hidden canyons, perfect for resting tired horses and changing brands on cattle. Anyone who wanted to disappear, could. And the honest homesteaders of the area turned a blind eye to the outlaws who used it as a haven.

In the mid-1890s, Hole-in-the-Wall served as the favorite hideout for the charming and good-natured Butch Cassidy, whose real name was Robert Leroy Parker. Parker had formed the gang known as the Wild Bunch when he teamed up with Kid Curry, an impassive, hardcore killer. Other members of the Hole-in-the-Wall gang included Harry Longbaugh, the Sundance Kid; Ben "the Tall Texan" Kilpatrick; the intelligent and educated Elza Lay; and several other men and women. One of the latter was an attractive, auburn-haired prostitute called Etta Place, who has been misrepresented as a lonely schoolteacher in stories and films.

Careful planning kept the gang out of jail most of the time. Cassidy believed in riding the best possible horses and arranged for relay stations with fresh mounts along escape routes. He himself never killed a man, although some of his cronies killed easily and often. In the 1889 train robbery at Wilcox, Wyoming, the gang added to its fame when Cassidy overused his dynamite, blowing $60,000 into the sky along with the door to the baggage car. The outlaws managed to gather up most of the loot, however. In the late-1890s, the Wild Bunch increased its take by successfully robbing a coal company paymaster and several trains.

Their successes led a posse hired by the Union Pacific railroad, as well as other lawmen in the region, to pursue them rigorously. So after the turn of the century, Cassidy, the Sundance Kid and Etta headed for South America. There the two men were reportedly shot to death in a battle with Bolivian soldiers. However, stories that the two managed to escape and returned to the United States have persisted to this day, adding to the legendary status of these devil-may-care outlaws.

The 1890s gave America one of its greatest outlaw legends: Butch Cassidy (seated right), the Sundance Kid (seated left) and The Wild Bunch.

(ABOVE) *A Hopi woman dresses the hair of an unmarried girl in the traditional manner.*

(RIGHT) *Native Americans in full regalia ride past the well-dressed people of Omaha, Nebraska, in an Indian Day Parade on August 4, 1898.*

THE VICTORIAN FAMILY

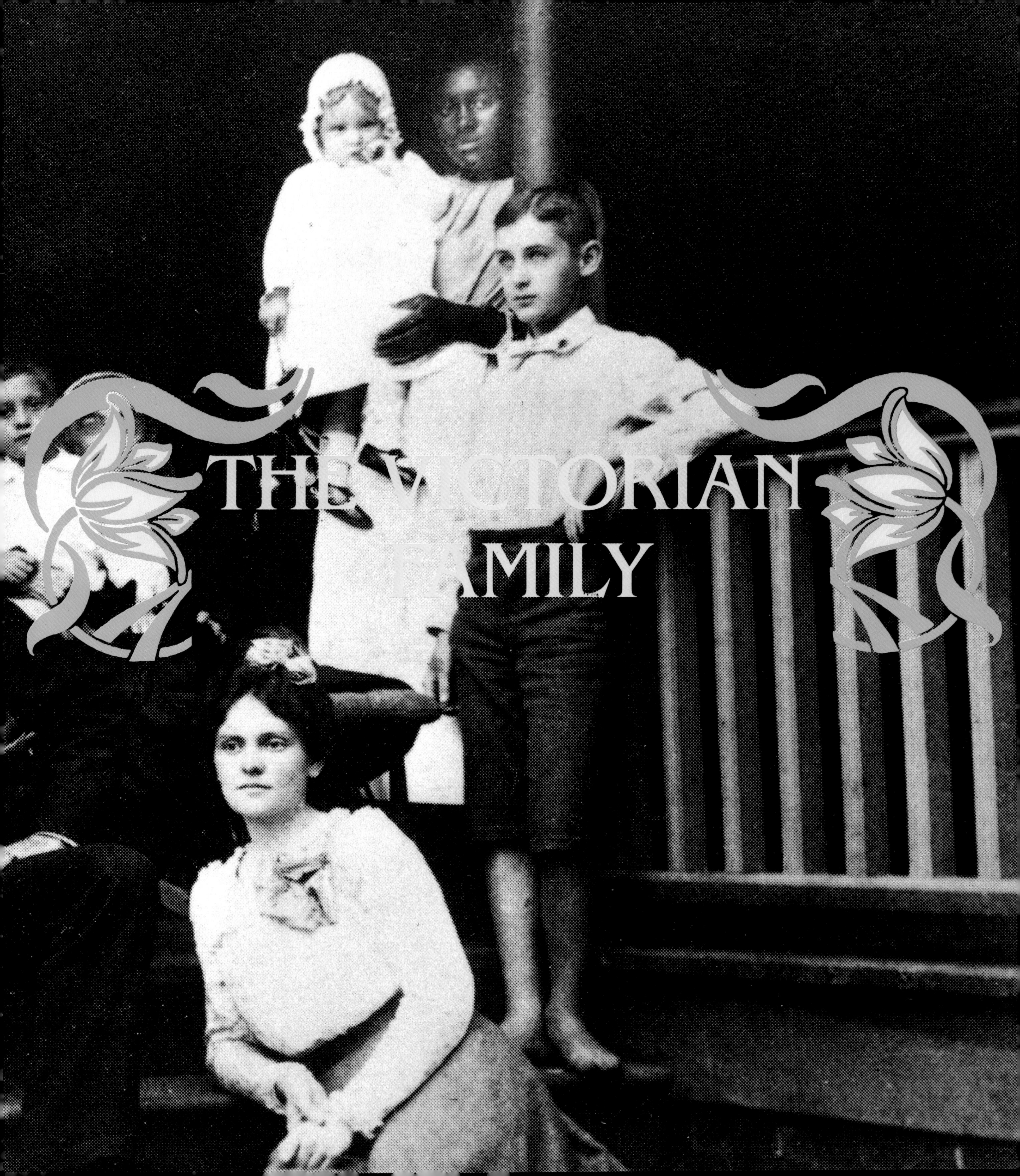

The Victorian Family

Americans viewed family life with a heavy dose of sentimentality in the 1890s, but the real American home differed greatly from the idealized perception. Indeed, family life had been undergoing profound changes since the early 1800s, as greater mobility and shifting work patterns had fostered new life-styles among men and women. By the end of the 19th century, many people were concerned over the growing independence of the lady of the house, as well as the trend toward smaller families and the various effects of urbanization on the home. In the 1890s, many experts proclaimed the American family in decline and proposed various cures, all aimed at the creation of a new ideal.

One of the realities of the day was the increasing separation of family members. Parents and their children had once labored together or in close proximity, but by the 1890s, most fathers worked long hours in factories or offices some distance away from their wives and children. Meanwhile, the women, keeping house in greater isolation from those around them in larger and more impersonal towns, assumed more and more of the responsibility for child rearing. Thus, where the child care books of the early 1800s had addressed "the parents," those in the 1890s spoke primarily to Mom, now charged with total responsibility for the development of her youngsters. Correspondingly, "the cult of motherhood" reached a pinnacle of sugary sentimentality during the decade, with "Mother" alternately seen as the civilizing force, the shaper of America's future, and the fountainhead of the home.

When she wasn't aspiring to such ethereal roles, the

This 1897 stereoptican slide entitled "The evening chapter" portrays one of the family's typical after-dinner recreational activities.

Dressed in their summer finery, this family of four in Kentucky posed for the camera in 1899.

wife and mother of the typical middle-class family was very busy. She spent many hours sewing everything from children's clothes to rugs and quilts; preparing elaborate meals; canning and preserving; and baking bread, cakes, and pies. In fact, baking and sewing were regarded as such important measures of a woman's domestic skill that even those with servants spent much of their day at such work. Servants were greatly desired when it came to washing and ironing, however. These time-consuming and onerous tasks were done by hand, usually twice a week. The newly invented washing machine was inefficient and sometimes leaked or tore clothes, so laundresses, who charged about $2 a load, were preferable.

For those who could afford it, the use of daily and live-in help was promulgated as a way of freeing women from household tasks so that they could perform charitable service work. But most women worked in partnership with servants, as the myriad tasks of running an 1890s home and raising children required the efforts of both parties.

(PREVIOUS PAGES) *In this turn-of-the-century portrait, Bishop Theodore Dubose Bratton is surrounded by his loved ones—including a goat—in Raleigh, North Carolina. Servants on the porch hold the youngest children.*

During the course of the decade, it became increasingly difficult to find household help, as the better-paying factory jobs lured people from low status domestic work.

It was an era in which the home was a place of refuge for the husband who faced the hard, competitive world of the workplace. The man of the house, charged with making as much money as possible, was invited to leave his money-grubbing ways behind at the end of the day and enter the woman's realm. In her efforts to create a "garden of peace and beauty" for herself and her breadwinner, the woman typically cultivated blooming and green plants. Palms and vases of flowers littered the living areas of the Victorian home. As apartment and hotel living became more prevalent, writers of the era bemoaned the passing of the garden home. Many issued dire warnings about the impact of apartment dwelling on the health of men, women, and especially children.

Indeed, children became the focus of new attention in the 1890s. Prevalent opinion of the day held that a child should be trained and educated from infancy onward. In keeping with this theory, the beginning of the decade saw the initiation of preschool education, or kindergarten, in several cities. These institutions promulgated the notion of combining "manual training with organized play." Children's toys and eating utensils also became educational tools: plates were decorated with the alphabet and maps, while puzzles, and card games informed youngsters about the world. "Sunday toys," like wooden Noah's Arks, miniature churches, and "Pilgrim's Progress" board games, instructed a child in Biblical subjects, thus making it possible for him or her to play on the Sabbath. Middle-class and upper-class children were dressed up and expected to behave like miniature men and women

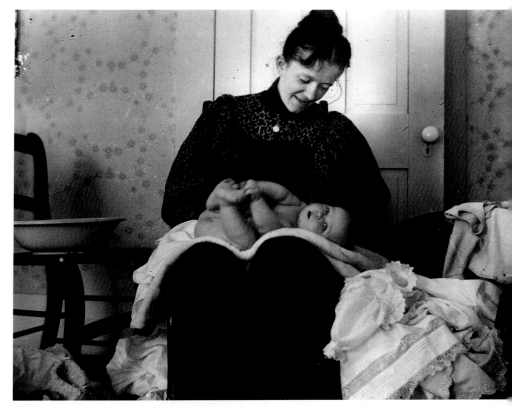

During the 1890s, child-rearing—formerly the responsibility of both parents—became primarily the province of the mother.

most of the time. A little girl's hair was often wound on bobs at night, so that she would have pretty ringlets the next day. Boys' and girls' formal clothes were stiff and ornate, and for special occasions the girl might wear heavy jewelry and a child's corset (corsets were designed for "infants to adults"). The decade saw a growing controversy about such practices, but the criticism was confusing to many ambitious mothers. Immersed in a society in which ostentation was everything, it seemed to them only right that their children should be decorated and displayed.

Manners and deportment were major issues between parents and children, and many magazine columns, books, and newspaper articles concentrated on the necessity of teaching a child to be polite in public—once again as a demonstration of the family's wealth and position. In fact, children of all backgrounds and income brackets tended to misbehave on many occasions, no matter how much "training" they had received.

As in any period of rapid change, the 1890s looked to the past for the ultimate ideal of domestic bliss, and many Americans longed for the large, extended family that had worked together in the good, old-fashioned way. But that family only fit into an agrarian, largely rural society. The industrial age demanded a new kind of family unit of which the Victorian household was the experimental model. Thus it was a family in transition, still containing remnants of the preindustrial age, yet with distinct changes in the roles and responsibilities of father, mother, and child.

As the decade wore on, it became increasingly difficult for ladies of means to find domestic help. In this stereoptican slide, the woman on the left is surprised to find her young helper scalloping oysters with a bowl and scissors.

113

(OPPOSITE) *This photo depicts three generations of a single family engaged in myriad pastimes in the parlor, including reading, playing with toys, and peering at pictures through a stereoptican viewer.*

 (RIGHT) *For those who could afford it, Edison's new-fangled home phonograph brought professional entertainment into the family home for the first time in history.*

 (BELOW) *In the days of rather constricting clothes and no air-conditioning, families often relaxed on the front porch at the end of the day.*

(BELOW) *The parlor of the Hoffman mansion in New York in 1899.*

(BOTTOM) *Frank Lloyd Wright's drafting studio in Oak Park, Illinois, typified the young, innovative architect's approach to interior design, one that offered a simple, uncluttered alternative to the prevailing style.*

Room for Excess

Today it's known as "Victorian clutter," but in the 1890s residential interiors crowded with heavy dark furniture were considered the ideal reflection of permanence and prosperity, while the display of multitudinous decorative objects was seen as an indication of culture and good taste. Thus, geegaws, bric-a-brac, souvenirs, and whatnots were juxtaposed against the busiest of floral wall paper and fabric-draped mantels and pianos. Good taste, as always, was a relative term.

The most important room of the house was the drawing room or parlor, where the family came together and the guests were entertained. Myriad treasures, from sea shells to statues, were displayed on small tables, shelves, and on the popular étagère, a cabinet consisting of open shelves. Just as empty space was abhorred on tabletop and floor, so too were blank walls. Hence, there was an abundance of oil portraits, landscapes, and prints hanging in every conceivable space.

Wealthy music hall star Lillian Russell showed off the current fads when she gave a tour of her new brownstone in 1893. In addition to enormous tigerskin rugs, leather-covered walls, and imposing fireplaces in various rooms, the parlor of her New York house was packed with stout chairs and divans, accented by Turkish pillows. Collections of souvenir spoons, snuffboxes, jeweled cigarette holders, miniature musical instruments, china, and medallions were reflected in a floor-to-ceiling mirror, and an incense burner imposed a smoky haze.

Although the public rooms of 1890s homes were the very definition of excess, bedrooms and the kitchen were rather subdued. Of course, because these rooms were rarely seen by outsiders, ostentation was pointless, but more importantly, the latest scientific theories suggested that these rooms were breeding grounds for infectious disease and as such were best kept clean and uncluttered.

Although Victorian ostentation was the order of the day, signs of change could be seen in the early work of Frank Lloyd Wright, whose Prairie School of architecture produced homes of substance and style (if not yet in the low, horizontal mode for which he would become famous). His interiors featured open, expansive spaces and the furniture, which he often designed himself, was relatively simple and elegant. The Arts and Crafts movement of the early 20th century would also help to change the look of middle-class American homes, but in most of the parlors and drawing rooms of the 1890s, fussiness and overcrowding still prevailed.

(OPPOSITE) *This hodgepodge of portraits and geegaws could easily be described as Victorian clutter.*

(RIGHT) *This stereoptican slide is meant to be humorous—the little girl is speaking into the listening piece—but it does illustrate the burgeoning importance of the telephone in the average family home.*

(OPPOSITE) *Dancing gave courting couples a rare opportunity for physical contact but smooching in public—as depicted in this staged photograph—would have been considered highly improper.*

(BELOW) *Domestic work was one of the few options generally open to women in the 19th century. Those who gave the "Gilded Age" its name employed fleets of servants. The Cornelius Vanderbilts, for example, had a domestic staff of 40 when they stayed at the Breakers, their Newport summer "cottage." They had an even larger staff for their New York home.*

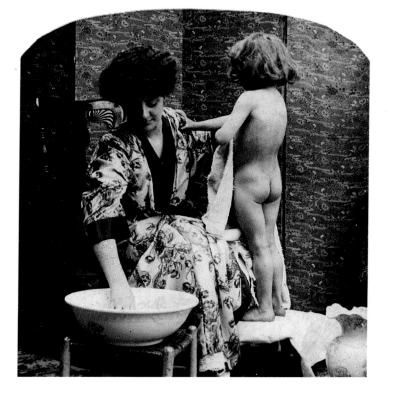

 (LEFT) *This tender photograph of a mother and child recalls the images of Impressionist painter Mary Cassatt, whose works were becoming popular during the 1890s. At the time, few homes had bathrooms so this child was probably bathed in the kitchen.*

(OPPOSITE) *It was an age of chauvinism. Father was the bread winner, and often ruled the Victorian household as a benevolent despot.*

(BELOW) *A woman's talent with a needle and thread was regarded as an important measure of her domestic skill. During the 1890s, most mothers made clothes for their families as well as curtains, blankets, and even tents for camping expeditions.*

(OPPOSITE LEFT) *Three Colorado children . . . and their dolls.*

 (OPPOSITE RIGHT) *The chaps on this African-American youngster, and his broad-brimmed hat, recall the attire of the performers in Buffalo Bill's Wild West Show. Perhaps he saw the Congress of Rough Riders when they played New York.*

(BELOW) *This is the 1893 kindergarten class of a school in Wilmington, Delaware, operated for the children of Joseph Bancroft & Sons' mill workers. Kindergarten was an 1890s innovation.*

High Society

One hundred years ago, the life-style of the very rich reached a level of isolated grandeur reminiscent of European royalty. Much of America's upper class was untouched by the era's economic hard times, and many of its members seemed obsessed with extremely conspicuous displays of their wealth. At one of Mrs. Astor's New York dinner parties, for example, the dinner table was covered with several inches of sand in which valuable jewels were buried. The famed society matron provided a sterling silver bucket and spade for each guest so that he or she could dig for party favors.

Clothes were another source of ostentation. It was said that the typical lady of society wore about $13,000 in gown and jewels (worth much more today, of course) when she attended the horse shows in the newly built Madison Square Garden.

The excesses of Mrs. Astor and other members of high society came to a climax in the great summer "cottages" built in Newport, Rhode Island, in the 1890s. Here, comfortable residences in the typical rambling Victorian style gave way to immense marble palaces patterned after French chateaux and Italianate palaces. The owners crammed as many priceless tapestries, paintings, and

objets d'art as their homes—some with as many as 70 rooms—could hold; a few commissioned life-size crucifixes to hang in the staircase halls.

During the long summer season at Newport, the lives of the very rich revolved around fashionable gatherings and the carriage parade that went along Bellevue Avenue and out on to Ocean Drive. Young ladies in lacy dresses and feathery hats flirted with the young men in the next carriage, while dowagers, rigidly upright in their whalebone corsets, supervised. In the afternoons, the outdoor types might be seen playing tennis at the Casino or luxuriating on the long, white yachts. Dinners were reportedly eaten off gold plates with a footman behind every chair.

Despite the grandeur of the parties and the amusing rivalries between the great ladies, cracks were appearing in the facade of high society by the turn of the century. As newspapers provided ordinary Americans with reports of their excessive life-style, public disapproval became loud enough that a few of the super rich took extended trips to Europe to escape the condemnation. It began to look as if high society would have to evolve, along with the rest of the culture. The times, indeed, were changing.

 (OPPOSITE) *In New York, the notoriously-wealthy Mrs. John Jacob Astor resided at Fifth Avenue and 64th Street (bottom). The Cornelius Vanderbilts weren't far away in their mansion on Fifth Avenue (top).*

 (LEFT) *George Vanderbilt spends a quiet moment alone with his daughter Cornelia. His mansion, Biltmore, in Asheville, North Carolina, was the largest private home in America.*

 (BELOW) *The William K. Vanderbilts had the most extravagant ballroom in Newport, Rhode Island. It was the showpiece of Marble House, the family's $11 million summer "cottage."*

Before the 20th century, large extended families lived together or in close proximity to one another. Here the women and children of a large Minnesota clan gather together before a strikingly patterned tarpaper house.

(ABOVE) *This Missouri couple, out for a Sunday ride in the park, seems half-surprised by the photographer's presence.*

(LEFT) *The parlor piano offered a socially-acceptable way for courting couples to enjoy a few moments of harmless physical proximity.*

Keeping Company

Roller skating, ice skating and bicycling—these were popular means of exercise in the last decade of the 19th century, but for young Americans, they represented significant opportunities, too. Skating gave couples a chance to hold hands in public and bicycling meant a boy and girl could pedal off in privacy.

Opportunities of that sort were greatly appreciated in an era dominated by the strictures of Victorian morality. Although the decade saw some relaxation in those strictures, courtship still had plenty of rules and regulations. For example, well-bred boys and girls weren't supposed to be alone together and it was highly improper for single people to address each other by their first names. And when a young man came to call, he typically brought

In the 1890s, courtship behavior was still somewhat old-fashioned: the male was supposed to be solicitous, attentive and agreeable to his lady love, and the lady very submissive.

flowers, candy, or a book.

Despite the conventions of the day, urban life afforded young adults brand new chances to bend the rules. Pianos—de rigeuer for the townhouse parlor—enabled courting couples to manage a bit of physical intimacy while playing duets. And the popular two-step brought dancers closer together. Even the living environment could bring one into new and exciting relationships with members of the opposite sex. In 1891, for example, John Franklin Jameson, a 32-year old professor in Providence, Rhode Island, courted a 26-year-old music teacher in the boardinghouse where they lived. He read poetry to her and flirted with her at the dinner table. Later, when he was separated from her during their engagement, Jameson wrote her letters on a "newfangled" typewriting machine and occasionally talked to her by telephone, a costly luxury but sometimes worth it when he felt compelled "to get [Sallie] up to a long-distancer, just to hear that dear sweet voice."

Thus, as more and more young people moved from the country to the city, the nature of romance began to change. Some of the changes meant more freedom—chaperoning became noticeably more lax as the decade went along—but other inhibitions just took on a new face. Dormitories and boardinghouses had strict rules and many a young man learned to dread the sight of a girlfriend's flinty eyed landlady, protective and proper as ten aunties.

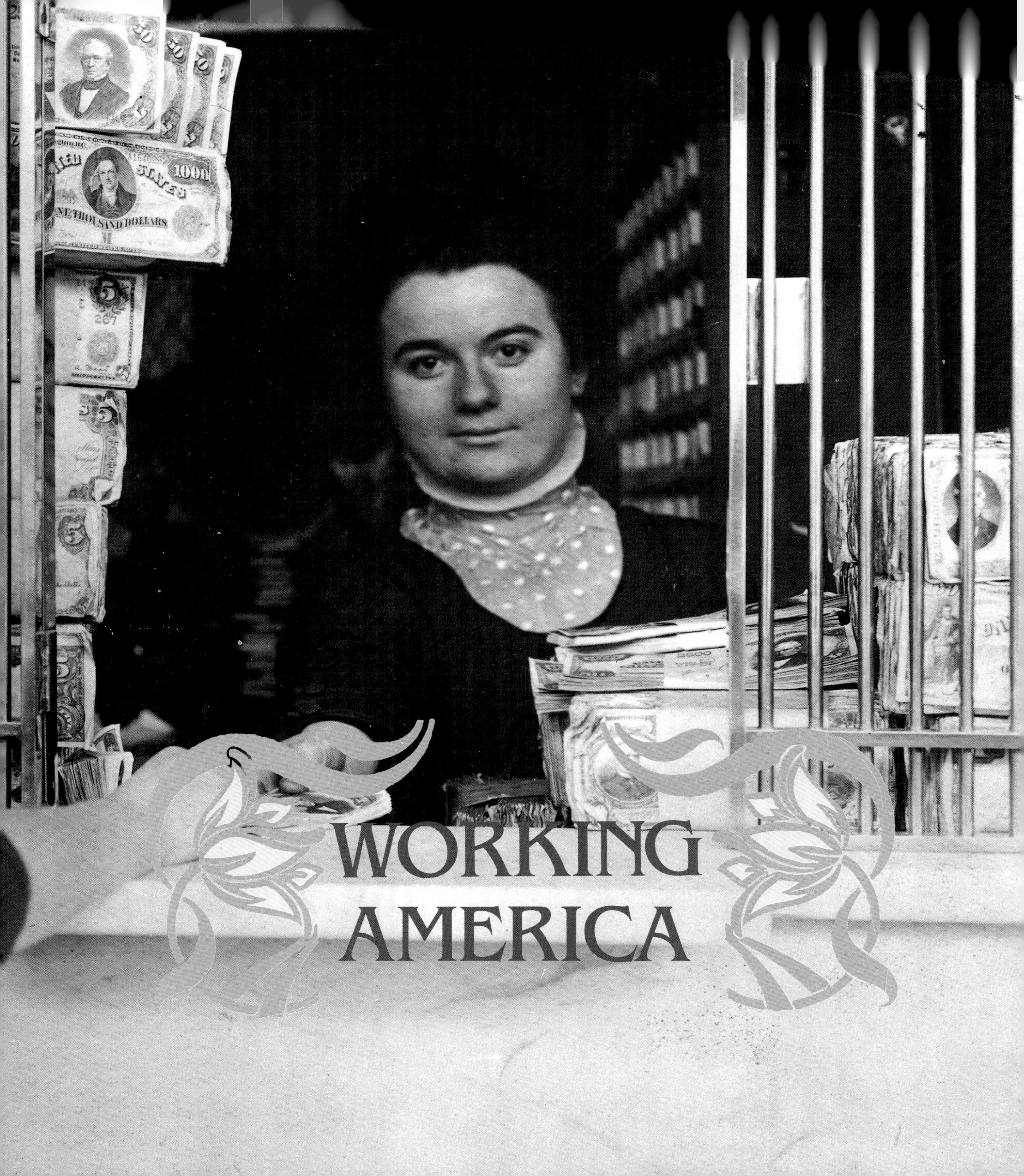

WORKING AMERICA

Working America

During the 20th century, government regulation of the workplace (including the establishment of a minimum wage), the rising power of the labor unions, and the concept of leisure time for all have radically changed the character of working America. Consequently, much that is taken for granted today simply didn't exist in the work place of the 19th century. When an American went to work in the 1890s, for example, there was no such thing as a five-day week. Most workers put in about 58 hours, and the average working day was about 10 hours long.

For most Americans at the end of the 19th century, agriculture still represented the primary means of earning a living. But that was changing. Whereas 16 percent of the nation's populace lived in urban environments before the Civil War, 40 percent were city dwellers by the turn of the century. This transition from a rural to an urban economy was the legacy of the Industrial Revolution—for the most part, people who stopped working on farms started working in large factories.

The change was especially noticeable in the South, where textile mills had been established in the two decades following the Civil War. Mill jobs were eagerly sought by young workers discouraged by the devastated farm economy and eager to sample the attractions of city life. Meanwhile, in the West and Midwest, mechanized farming led to increased productivity while reducing the requisite number of field hands. Corn planters, potato planters, mowing machines, and combines, which reaped, threshed, cleaned, and bagged grain, were changing the face of agriculture. In 1850, for example, it

The White Oak Cotton Mills in Greensboro, North Carolina.

took 21 hours to harvest a ton of hay; by the end of the 1890s, it took only four.

During the decade, actual wages for most jobs shrank, with the average worker earning 20 cents an hour and unskilled laborers receiving less. In addition, long layoffs were common, so that only a few people worked all year. Families compensated for the inadequate wages as they always had, by putting their children to work. Indeed, large numbers of young people were employed in factories, in the fields, and in cottage industries at home, and they were expected to put in the same long hours as adults, but for less pay.

Still, for many households, even those with every family member at work, earning a living wage was difficult. Management maintained that workers needed to work harder. Others simply believed that there would always be poor people. Regardless of the reasons, estimates indicated that at the end of the 1890s, more than 10 million working Americans were not earning enough to support themselves. As a result, the decade saw increasingly trou-

(PREVIOUS PAGES) *This photograph, taken in around 1890, is labeled "The only woman bank cashier in America, or possibly the world."*

A "doffer" in a textile mill in Augusta, Georgia.

On opposite sides of the biggest labor-management dispute of the age were (left) Eugene Debs, American socialist and union leader, and (right) George Pullman, American industrialist and inventor.

The steel mogul and philanthropist, Andrew Carnegie.

bled relations between labor and management. Strikes became more common and two of the most controversial disputes illustrated the major issues of the times.

The first came in 1892, when workers struck Andrew Carnegie's steel plant in Homestead, Pennsylvania. The president of the company, Henry Frick, was strongly opposed to organized labor, and he refused to negotiate with members of an iron and steel workers union that had protested the company's 12-hour work shifts. Instead he hired strikebreakers with 300 armed Pinkerton detectives for protection. A gun battle ensued, federal troops were called in, and ultimately, the union was destroyed. In a letter to Carnegie, Frick wrote, "We had to teach our employees a lesson, and we have taught them one they will never forget."

Two years later, a strike occurred that the *New York Times* called the greatest battle between labor and capital ever seen in the United States. George M. Pullman had grown enormously wealthy by manufacturing the Pullman car, a special sleeping car for trains. In 1893, his company was paying its stockholders very well. Despite this prosperity, however, Pullman suddenly laid off almost half his work force and slashed the wages of some 3,000 workers who remained. When his employees attempted to talk with him to discuss the cuts, he politely refused to hold a meeting. The workers lived in the Pullman company town, and despite the pay cut, there was no reduction in the high rent on houses or in the exorbitant prices at the company store. Finally, faced with few options the workers struck. Their actions had little effect until the American Railway Union, under the leadership of its president, Eugene V. Debs, decided not to operate any train that had a Pullman sleeping car attached to it. When switchmen who refused to handle sleepers were fired, other railroad workers began to walk off the job in sympathy. Within a few days, it was obvious that the American Railway Union was winning the strike—

the North was virtually paralyzed and thousands of people were wearing white armbands in sympathy. However, the U.S. attorney general's sympathies were with the railroads, and he threw all his weight into breaking the strike through court injunctions. When these efforts failed, President Grover Cleveland sent federal troops to Chicago to "settle" the dispute.

Meanwhile, violence and mayhem spread to other cities across the country, as armed militia fired on many Americans and arrested thousands. When the strike was finally crushed in August 1894, it was estimated that property damage ran into the millions. Approximately 25 strikers were killed and 60 seriously injured. The workers didn't win any concessions from Pullman, but they won the public's sympathy.

Americans began to realize the extent of the working person's problems and his or her helplessness in an industrial society. They saw that in the new workplace—in a factory, a large farm, or a corporate office—an enormous distance separated the worker from the boss. To bridge this gulf, laborers increasingly sought strength in numbers. By the late 1890s, the American Federation of Labor, a group of unions that had banded together in the 1880s, had added hundreds of thousands of members to its roster. By decade's end, some progressive industrialists saw that unless salaries and conditions improved, militants might stir thé already disgruntled workers to violent rebellion. The federal government, perhaps to set a positive example, mandated an eight-hour day for its employees.

Thus, as far as the workplace was concerned, the 1890s were a rather somber decade. But it left the working people more determined than ever to solve the problems of, and improve the working conditions in, this newly industrialized society.

(OPPOSITE) *For those who couldn't find regular employ-ment or who needed a source of supplementary income, the home became a workplace, as seen in the family sewing piece goods in their kitchen-living room (top) and the Italian family assembling artificial flowers at their kitchen table (bottom).*

 (BELOW) *Two workers at a lathe in a machine shop. The man on the right is too well dressed to be a laborer. Perhaps he is inspecting the equipment or instructing the man at left.*

America's premiere labor leader, Samuel Gompers.

 (ABOVE) *Young textile workers on strike in Philadelphia, just like adults.*

 (OPPOSITE) *A young girl wistfully gazes out the window of the textile mill where she works. She put in the same long hours as an adullt, but for less pay.*

The Workingman's Friend

Like many immigrant children, Samuel Gompers began working when he was 10 years old. By the time he was was 17 and married, he could look forward to a life of endless toil as a cigar maker. But the energetic and gregarious Gompers had ambitions.

Outside the sweat shop, he studied political science and economy and joined unions and lodges, getting to know his fellow workers. In 1886, he helped establish the American Federation of Labor, a coalition of craft unions with one overriding goal: improving the working conditions of industrial workers. In the 1890s, Gompers began to take a leading role in the union—under his influence, the A.F. of L. avoided political alliances, social reform, and radicalism, and in fact, strongly supported capitalism.

"Our labor movement has no system to crush," he said. By steering his union away from extremist positions, Gompers averted attacks from the police and kept public sympathy on labor's side. However, the resolute Gompers did not shy away from strikes and boycotts, which he used in the fight for shorter hours and better wages. He also influenced legislation to abolish child labor. Gompers pursued his goals in a no-nonsense and courageous manner that won grudging admiration. But the pragmatic leader did not try to better working conditions for everyone: the A.F. of L. only admitted craftsmen to the organization, shutting out unskilled laborers. Skilled workers were, in fact, only a small percentage of the labor force at the time, and they opposed spreading benefits to outsiders.

By the turn of the century, Gompers led a union with a membership of over half a million workers. For forty years, he was America's most influential labor leader, and he is often credited with preventing outright war between American industry and its sometimes unhappy work force.

Out of the Home and Into the Workplace

While farm women in Ohio slopped the hogs, and recently arrived immigrant women in New York sat at home making artificial flowers, thousands of other women around the United States were going to work in factories. By 1900, four times as many women were working in industry as had been doing so 30 years earlier. New York's Rose Schneiderman, who later became a labor leader, worked as a cap maker in the 1890s, when sixty hours of stitching paid about five dollars a week. In addition to the long hours and low pay, it was customary in the garment trade for the working woman to buy her own machine, paying it off gradually out of meager wages. But Rose and others were proud of their labor. Morever, work provided them with a chance to escape restrictive family environments. Friendships and romances flourished in the factories.

Of course, different strata of society were restricted in the types of work they could do. Thus, African-American women, who worked outside the home in much greater numbers than their white counterparts, were employed largely as domestic servants. Meanwhile, young middle-class women found themselves working as clerks and office workers—especially as "typewriters" (in the 1890s,

that was the designation for those who worked the machine as well as the machine itself). And they were breaking down the barriers in the professions. Although a few law schools were still closed to females, the number of women who became teachers, nurses, librarians, and social workers skyrocketed.

One age-old job was readily available to the young, urban woman with no skills: prostitution. Although reformers worked hard to eliminate such a livelihood during the 1890s, it nevertheless presented an alternative to the grueling work available to women in need—and paid about five times the average wage.

There was serious opposition to women in the work force. Only two national unions even admitted females to their ranks. "The growing demand for female labor is . . . an insidious assault upon the home . . .," said one labor leader, accusing the working woman of "displacing the father, brother, and son." Whether or not anyone approved, women were in the workplace to stay. They comprised only about 17 percent of working America in the 1890s, but their influence and numbers were growing.

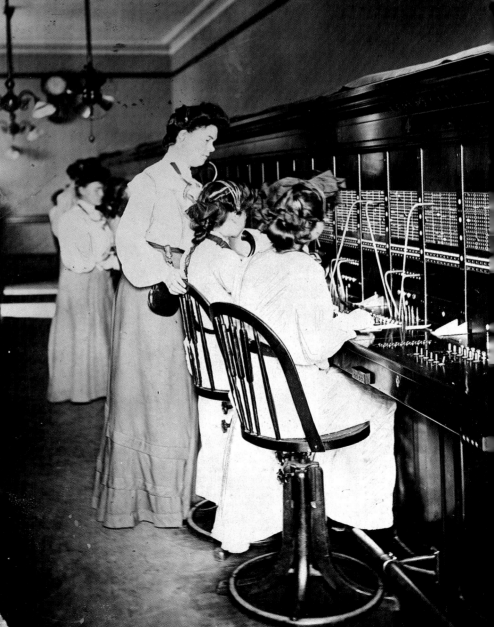

 (ABOVE) *This humorous photograph illustrates the easy workload of an office clerk, thanks to the recent advent of the portable typewriter.*

 (RIGHT) *From the beginning of the telephone system, women worked as operators. This photo shows a switchboard in around 1890.*

(OPPOSITE) *Women workers count and sort new dollar bills at the U.S. Treasury in Washington, D. C.*

(PRECEEDING PAGES) *The Pioneer Sheridan Hose was a well-organized volunteer unit in Sheridan, Wyoming, when this photo was taken in 1893. The wooden structures of most Western towns, and their close proximity to one another, made the work of fire brigades a vital public service.*

With the advent of industrialization, new jobs and new types of jobs were emerging. At the same time, some traditional forms of labor were starting to disappear . . .

 (OPPOSITE TOP) *Motorized transport would soon make horse-drawn freight wagons—and the men who drove them—products of a bygone age.*

(OPPOSITE BOTTOM) *Scissors and knives became increasingly inexpensive thanks to mass production. The itinerant knife and scissors grinder, such as the one seen here in Atlanta, Georgia, would no longer be needed. One would simply buy new utensils when the old ones became dull.*

(BELOW) *For centuries, the village blacksmith had been on hand to forge tools, create replacement parts, and shoe horses. Mass production and the invention of the automobile would render these roles redundant within a few years of the taking of this photo in 1890.*

 (TOP) *African-Americans selling fish at a market in New Jersey in 1896.*

(ABOVE) *Lumberjacks slowly work their way through a massive felled tree in Minnesota.*

 (LEFT) *The interior of the Ontario Mine in Utah.*

145

Hard Times

For many Americans, the first sign of something really wrong came when those ominous "blue tickets" appeared in their pay envelopes. These layoff notifications multiplied quickly, as factory smokestacks across the Northeastern manufacturing region stopped smoking.

There had been monetary uncertainty since the outset of the decade, when the passage of the Sherman Silver Law enabled bearers of silver certificates to redeem their holdings for gold. The resultant run on the bullion of the U.S. Treasury brought gold reserves to a dangerous low. Meanwhile, international speculators began withdrawing funds from their American investments as they sensed a downturn in the U.S. economy. In something of a self-fulfilling prophecy, the crisis of confidence led to the stock market crash of June 1893, and the worst depression since the 1870s swept the United States.

During the Panic of 1893, nearly 500 banks closed and 16,000 businesses failed; even those who kept their jobs saw wage cuts of as much as 50 percent. Farmers out West found themselves caught in the three-way trap of falling farm prices, high railroad shipping charges, and no credit.

Bread lines and soup kitchens appeared everywhere, and suddenly there were men tramping over the land—thousands of them—trying to find someplace to work. General Jacob Coxey organized some of the men for a march on Washington, a "petition in boots" to draw attention to their plight and to demand help from national leaders. The idealistic general had hoped to lead 100,000 of the dispossessed and jobless, but Coxey's Army contained fewer than 1,000 by the time it reached Washington. Moreover, upon arrival in the nation's capitol, Coxey was arrested and his followers dispersed.

Some cities created public works projects and a morass of public and private programs arose, but they were insufficient and uncoordinated, because there were no federal agencies to organize the isolated efforts. Although many congressmen were sympathetic to the plight of their constituents, the prevailing belief was that these problems were outside government jurisdiction—and that the fittest would survive. Many middle-class and upper-class Americans feared an armed rebellion by the unemployed, but they did not recognize a fundamental factor underlying the situation: hope. The structure of U.S. society at the time, although not altogether open, allowed a chance for advancement. During the mid-1890s, the unemployed workers continued to hang on, with the conviction that, in the end, hard times would end and they would once more have a chance for a place in the sun.

 (ABOVE) *Many unemployed workers were forced to live in hovels and shacks as a result of the severe Depression of 1893. Scenes like this one recall the more familiar "Hoovervilles" of the 1930s.*

(RIGHT) *Gen. Jacob Coxey hoped to lead an army of unemployed workers on Washington, D.C. to draw attention to their plight. Instead, he and two of his associates were arrested for walking on the grass surrounding the national capitol.*

(OPPOSITE) *A long line—consisting primarily of women— forms outside a bank at 4th Avenue and 14th Street in New York. It was closed by the state.*

 (FOLLOWING PAGES) *Bicycle manufacturing was a new and booming industry in the 1890s. This factory was in Hartford, Connecticut.*

THE GROWING
METROPOLIS

The Growing Metropolis

The elevated railroad transformed the city of New York.

People of all classes and backgrounds gradually began to realize that life in the metropolis—fueled by an explosion of population and technology, fired in the industrial furnace, and tempered by reform—required innovative thinking. Americans, with characteristic energy and enthusiasm, threw themselves into the experiment.

The metropolis had begun its metamorphosis in the 1870s. Before then, the nation's leading cities had been bustling commercial centers with economies typically based on agricultural commodites. For the most part, these centers were relatively small. People walked to many places on foot. Residences and shops intermingled. And the ethnically homogeneous citizens knew their neighbors.

After the Civil War, the effects of the Industrial Revolution began to alter the American cities, with manufacturing supplanting agriculture as the primary economic base. Hoards of people streamed into burgeoning urban centers to fill the jobs that emerging industries created. Consequently, apartments and tenements sprouted up, business districts developed, and telephones, trolleys, and electric lights proliferated.

Because there was no model for this kind of city and few attempts to plan its development, the results were, at best, mixed. By the 1890s, Americans were taking a long, hard look at the emerging metropolises—and they didn't like what they saw.

In fact, one of the major complaints concerned the unattractive appearance of the cities. Thus, progressive architects, designers, and interested amateurs sought to replace the dark, intricate, European-based Victorian style that had dominated urban architecture with a classical, streamlined look. This new style was given impetus by the likes of Richard Morris Hunt in the utopian White City built for the 1893 World Columbian Exhibition in Chicago. Indeed, the White City marked the beginning of the City Beautiful movement, which would come into its own in the early 20th century.

In the 1890s, City Beautiful advocates touted the idea of spectacular civic centers and gracious courtyards, malls, and parks as necessary accessories for the mature metropolis. They believed that beautification was valuable not only for aesthetic reasons, but to inspire the poorer residents to higher levels of achievement.

As cities attempted to dress themselves up, they simultaneously tried to clean up. And no wonder. In *Life on the Mississsippi*, Mark Twain had disparaged the condition of New Orleans's thoroughfares, bluntly stating, "The dust, waste-paper littered, was still deep in the streets." Other

The American city of the 1890s was a grand experiment with developers and architects exploring new forms for human interaction, like the shopping arcade, which opened in Cleveland in 1890. Steel-frame skyscrapers were also a new phenomenon, sparked by Chicago architect Louis Sullivan whose 11-story Wainwright Building was completed in St. Louis in 1891, followed by his 14-story Guaranty Trust Building in Buffalo in 1895. Meanwhile, the working poor were attempting to survive among crowded tenements and teeming streets, while the middle class found an alternative life-style, commuting on trolleys to and from "garden homes" outside the central city. The wealthiest urbanites—like the Vanderbilts and the Astors—promoted the idea of green belts and parks—then built small palaces overlooking them.

(PREVIOUS PAGES) *A view of New York's Fifth Avenue at Madison Square in 1899.*

large cities were just as filthy. Reformers in the more progressive urban centers began placing rubbish baskets on streets and organizing "clean-up days." In New York City, sanitation workers donned neat, white uniforms and became an efficient army.

The installation of brilliant electric street lights also transformed the big cities of the 1890s. Although gas illumination was still used in shop windows and on some streets, Edison's incandescent lamp (patented in 1880) not only brightened many a city thoroughfare, it also reduced the risk of fire that gas had presented. Continuing a program that had started during the 1880s, the decade saw cities replacing the forest of overhead electric, telegraph, and telephone wires with underground cables. Roadways also improved. As the rage for bicycling spurred the need for smooth streets, cities replaced cobblestone and gravel with paved thoroughfares of concrete and asphalt. Maintaining smooth streets was problematic in many cities, however, because competing street car companies were constantly installing more tracks.

By 1900, nearly every American city with a population of 25,000 or more had at least one electric trolley line. The electrified streetcars were faster, smoother, and cleaner than their horse-drawn predecessors, and at first they were seen as the ultimate answer to urban transportation needs. But in the 1890s, cities with myriad streetcar lines—Chicago had 15 separate trolley companies, for example—often experienced more chaos than convenience. The constant laying of lines blocked traffic for weeks. And when the first automobiles appeared toward the end of the decade, street congestion became a real problem, as the two forms of transportation competed for available space. Accidents between cars and trolleys were frequent; because the former were clearly here to stay, grumpy editorials about the latter began to appear in metropolitan newspapers.

The Arts Building at the Chicago Columbian Exposition of 1893. The fair's White City had a dramatic impact upon the look of urban America.

Some early urban planners saw subways as the real solution to the traffic problem. Officials and investors in certain cities agreed, and the first American subway opened in Boston in 1897; construction on systems in New York and Philadelphia began shortly thereafter.

Urban planning was still in its infancy in this decade, but reformers, city officials, and businessmen were beginning to coordinate efforts to improve the growing cities. There were, of course, nearly as many opinions on how to accomplish this goal as there were city dwellers. Despite the nearly overwhelming nature of the situation, most Americans believed that urban life was perfectable, however, and no longer viewed the metropolis as "civilization's inferno."

Architect Louis H. Sullivan pioneered the development of the steel-frame skyscraper in the 1890s.

The traffic jam, a typically 20th-century phenomenon, had its beginnings in the 1890s, as this photo of Chicago's Randolph and Dearborn Streets dramatically illustrates.

The Great American City

New York City emerged as a world-class metropolis and America's most extraordinary urban achievement in the 1890s. It kicked off the decade with the construction of the tallest building in the world at that time, the 309-foot Pulitzer Building and followed up with the opening of two new arts and entertainment centers, Madison Square Garden and Carnegie Hall. By the end of the decade, skyscrapers filled the central business district, and the city had annexed Brooklyn, the Bronx, Queens, and Staten Island—boosting its population to nearly 3½ million people.

New York had been a healthy and successful city throughout the 19th century and was already established as an important seaport and railroad center when the technological advances of the 1880s—the Brooklyn Bridge, the elevated railroads, and the development of the steel-framed skyscraper—sparked a period of enormous economic and population growth. The burgeoning cultural scene and the distinctive architectural styles of the new monuments and buildings helped foster an atmosphere of excitement and optimism.

However, this atmosphere was acquired at a considerable price. Miserable living conditions resulted from overcrowding. In parts of the city, population density reached 986 people per acre, a higher rate than that which existed in notoriously congested Bombay, where 760 people per acre prevailed.

Dirt, danger, and noise characterized daily life, as horses deposited about 2.5 million pounds of manure on the streets each day, and the new trolleys, which transported thousands daily, clanged through the streets at high speed. In fact, the practice of avoiding reckless motormen on Brooklyn's trolleys gave rise to the nickname for the borough's baseball team, the Dodgers.

Nonetheless, immigrants, artists, and wealthy entrepeneurs continued to stream into the city, and the buildings went higher and higher. No city has ever undergone such a visible transformation in so short a time as did New York in the last decade of the 19th century.

The development of the steel-frame skyscraper revolutionized the look of America's cities . . .

 (CENTER) *Atlanta's Equitable Building, which opened in 1892, was initially considered an eccentric experiment, but the structure, designed by the Chicago firm of Burnham & Root, became a success both economically and as a work of art.*

 (ABOVE) *Hailed as an architectural landmark, the Wainwright Building in St. Louis, Missouri, was designed by Louis Sullivan and completed in 1891.*

 (OPPOSITE) *Holabird & Roche's Tacoma Building stood at the Northeast corner of LaSalle and Madison Streets in Chicago, Illinois. The building was demolished in 1929.*

(RIGHT) *In Atlanta, Georgia, Grant Park was created at the behest of L. P. Grant who gave the city 100 acres for the project in 1883. This 1890 photo shows the north end of Lake Abana, where couples could enjoy a few moments alone in a rented canoe.*

 (BELOW) *Central Park, designed by Frederick Law Olmstead, was a masterpiece of urban planning and design, a peaceful oasis for New Yorkers set in the heart of Manhattan. Here strollers enjoy a Sunday afternoon in the Mall in 1894.*

 (OPPOSITE) *A pigtailed girl and her family look out over an idyllic scene near the Conservatory in San Francisco's Golden Gate Park.*

The Northeast

 (OPPOSITE TOP) *The Fairmount Water Works, Philadelphia.*

 (OPPOSITE BOTTOM) *The Faneuil Hall Market in Boston, Massachusetts.*

 (BELOW) *Broad Street in Philadelphia, Pennsylvania. City Hall, topped by a massive statue of William Penn, is at the terminus of the street.*

The Midwest

 (OPPOSITE) *A residential section of Chicago, Illinois, in 1893.*

 (BELOW) *Fourth and Market Streets in St. Louis, Missouri, at the turn of the century.*

The West

🎴 (ABOVE) *Market Street in San Francisco, California.*

🎴 (OPPOSITE) *This photograph of Salt Lake City is labeled "Laying the Capstone of the Great Temple" and is dated April 6, 1892.*

THE GREAT TEMPLE AT SALT LAKE CITY, UTAH. APRIL 6th 1892

(RIGHT) *The corner of Second South and Main in St. Lake City, Utah. The construction of trolley tracks caused an increasing amount of congestion and disruptions to urban life by the turn of the century.*

(BELOW) *Trolleys moved a growing number of people down Pennsylvania Avenue in Washington, D.C.*

(BOTTOM) *The need for mass transit in New York is illustrated by the number of people trying to get on this elevated train.*

166

Saving the Cities

In the 1890s, the rapidly worsening conditions of America's poor gave rise to a movement for urban reform. One of the most effective documents in that burgeoning crusade was Jacob Riis's *How the Other Half Lives*, published in 1890. Riis, a Danish immigrant himself, took readers inside blocks of tenements with names like Poverty Gap and Murderers' Alley, and showed them those who dwelled there, mostly immigrants, who were raising families in the midst of filth, fear, and darkness.

Most Americans were genuinely horrified to discover the misery in their midst, but they were also somewhat frightened by the potential for violence presented by millions of alienated, poverty-stricken people. Because there were no government programs to help clean up the slums and existing charities were inadequate, American reformers effectively used public outrage to gain official recognition of the crisis.

Settlement homes, like Jane Addams's Hull House, became the cornerstone of the movement. Hull House, established in Chicago in the late 1880s, provided educa-

tion, recreation, and a sense of belonging for the inner-city poor. The settlement workers, idealistic, middle-class men and women who had abandoned their own comfortable lifestyles to work in the tenement districts, became increasingly adept at publicizing the crisis, spearheading campaigns for new laws, and learning how to lobby city officials, legislators, and even U.S. presidents. Hull House became a model for the nation and the entire world during this period, and settlement houses spread to major cities throughout the nation, increasing from 6 in 1891 to 74 in 1897.

The reform movement focused on three major issues: the social and economic plight of the poor, the deterioration of morals, and the physical blight of the cities. During the decade, many activists came to believe that housing reform was the key to all other improvement. Although there was open disagreement on that point and others, the reform movement began to have a noticeable and positive effect on the urban crisis of the 1890s.

 (OPPOSITE) *Jacob Riis used photography to draw attention to the plight of the urban poor. This elderly woman, for example, is doing bead work (while smoking a pipe) in a depressing, crowded tenement room in about 1890.*

 (BELOW) *The prototype for most settlement homes was this one, Chicago's Hull House.*

(BELOW) *Street urchins seem to be aimlessly loitering behind a New York tenement building in this photo by Jacob Riis, circa 1890.*

Jane Addams, reformer and founder of Hull House.

Just for Fun

The twin forces of urbanization and rapidly advancing technology helped shape a new preoccupation with sports and recreation in the 1890s. Moving pictures of athletic events attracted a large audience to hitherto unknown forms of competition, and many people became avid readers of sports stories in the increasingly sophisticated newspaper and magazine coverage of the day. At the same time, the 1890s city dweller began to take an interest in his own physical development, recognizing the mostly sedentary nature of the urban life-style. Some people joined sports clubs, some took up outdoor hobbies, and some just found a good time wherever they could. Even in remote rural regions, people were able to enjoy an increasing array of carnivals and circuses that came rolling in on the newly laid railroad tracks. In general, however, the hinterlands lagged behind the rest of the country in sports and recreation, and some historians believe that this dearth helped fuel the growing discontent with agricultural life during the decade.

Meanwhile in town, middle-class folk bicycled and danced the most popular step of the day, the two-step, the

This six-some—in matching outfits—is ready to begin.

"After the Bath" was the title for this 1898 photo by W. B. Davidson, taken at the pier in Narraganset, Rhode Island.

COPYRIGHT 1898
BY
W. B. DAVIDSON.

wealthy flocked to horse shows and horse races, and progressive women removed their corsets to play tennis and golf. Ironically, many of the city dweller's activities were an unconscious re-creation of the more enjoyable aspects of rural life. Those who went boating, picnicking, and promenading in the park as a respite from crowded streets and constricted workplaces were, in their own way, simulating the activities of country folk, who of necessity took care of animals and plants and walked or rode horses to town.

The single most popular form of fresh-air exercise was the bicycle. Urbanites took up the craze by the thousands, as they climbed aboard single-, double-, and triple-seaters. Ultimately, the police were forced to ticket daredevil "blazers" who raced through the crowded streets, threatening the safety of pedestrians. More serious cyclists formed associations and touring clubs, whose members vigorously set out to establish new speed records.

The young women of the 1890s broke new ground in their pursuit of physical exercise, forming, among other things, the first girl's baseball team at the onset of the decade. In fact, women of all ages were proving that females could perform athletically. A case in point was middle-aged scholar Annie Smith Peck who climbed the

(PREVIOUS PAGES) *Whether by bicycle, carriage, or horseless carriage, pleasure-seekers found a way to reach the beach at Seabreeze, Florida.*

15,000-foot Matterhorn in 1895. The 45-year-old Peck said that it had only required "a little physical endurance, a good deal of brains, lots of practice and plenty of warm clothing." She continued climbing for 40 years.

The 1890s, in general, was an age of organization, and, when it came to sports, Americans formed athletic clubs and leagues at an unprecedented rate. The Young Men's Christian Associations were the major centers for organized team competition, including basketball, which was invented in 1891 by a YMCA instructor, Dr. James Naismith. Volleyball was another sport that got its start under a YMCA roof when William G. Morgan created the game in 1895. That year also saw an important milestone in football. It seems that the organizer of the YMCA team in Latrobe, Pennsylvania, Dave Berry, had been planning a particular game for months. A few days before kickoff, however, he lost his quarterback. In desperation, he contacted John Brallier, whom he'd never seen play, and offered him $10 to become a substitute quarterback. Thus, Brallier officially became the first professional football player in the history of the sport. That honor was of little consequence to the boy, however. When he arrived in Latrobe the night before the game, he told Berry how thrilled he was to see paved streets and wear long pants for the first time.

Physical education was also widely promoted in schools during the 1890s. Among other things, the decade saw the establishment of an on-going gridiron tradition, the Army-Navy game, first played at West Point on November 29, 1890. Navy won, 24-0. But not everything was always on the up and up. Rumor has it that seven members of the University of Michigan football squad of 1893 were not even students!

Elsewhere during the decade, court tennis gained popularity, spreading from Boston and Newport to New York City's Racquet and Tennis Club in 1891 and to the Chicago Athletic Club two years later. Ice hockey made its way from Canada to the United States, where it was played at Yale and Johns Hopkins Universities. Meanwhile, back in Canada, Lord Stanley of Preston, the nation's governor general, introduced a cup named for him in 1893, which became the game's professional championship trophy. The first national fly-casting tournament was held at the World's Columbian Exposition in 1893, the first U.S. Open Golf tournament was held in Newport, Rhode Island, in 1895, and the running of the first Boston Marathon came in 1897. Perhaps the most significant athletic event of the decade was the summer Olympics, a revival of the games of ancient Greece. In 1896, they were held in Athens— naturally—for the first time in the modern era.

Meanwhile, a dramatic increase in the media coverage of sports introduced masses of people to unknown athletic events and riveting accounts of physical prowess. *Century* magazine, for example, serialized a stirring, first-person chronicle by Captain Joshua Slocum, who in 1895 single-handedly circumnavigated the globe in his 37-foot sloop, *Spray*—the world's first such successful undertaking. An 1891 account of a ski journey across Greenland caused such an explosion of interest in this snow-based mode of human transport that eventually a new sport—downhill skiing—was established. In the meantime, however, winter enthusiasts contented themselves with the era's most popular forms of cold-air recreation—ice skating, sleigh riding, and sledding.

Boating on Loch Mary in Hopkins County, Kentucky, circa 1892.

In addition to newspapers and magazines, new forms of communication drew attention to sports and recreation. A photographer named Eadweard Muybridge produced sequential action photographs of race horses, baseball pitchers, and track events that revealed heretofore unknown aspects of motion and increased our knowledge of the workings of the human body. Motion pictures discovered boxing early on, with such novelties as a peep show image of a pugilist and the 1895 "flicker" of a six-round bout between Young Griffo and Battling Barnett. The finish of the America's Cup yacht race of 1899 was reported on Marconi's newly invented wireless.

By the turn of the century, Americans of all classes and types were more competitive, more active, and more interested in sports than ever before. Some believed that this mania for athletics had a deeper meaning. Because its rise was concurrent with the closing of the frontier, there were those like historian Frederic Logan Paxson who argued that sports had replaced the open, expansive West as a safety valve for Americans discontented with their lives, that athletics provided an escape from the unpleasant side of industrial society and dimmed thoughts of "revolution."

In any event, the new age of sports had a definitely positive effect on the American people. As a sportswriter of the time said, "An enormmous change for the better has taken place . . . [and] the result is seen in the glorious physical development of the young men and women whom we meet everywhere."

The Felts family picnic in Silver City, Idaho.

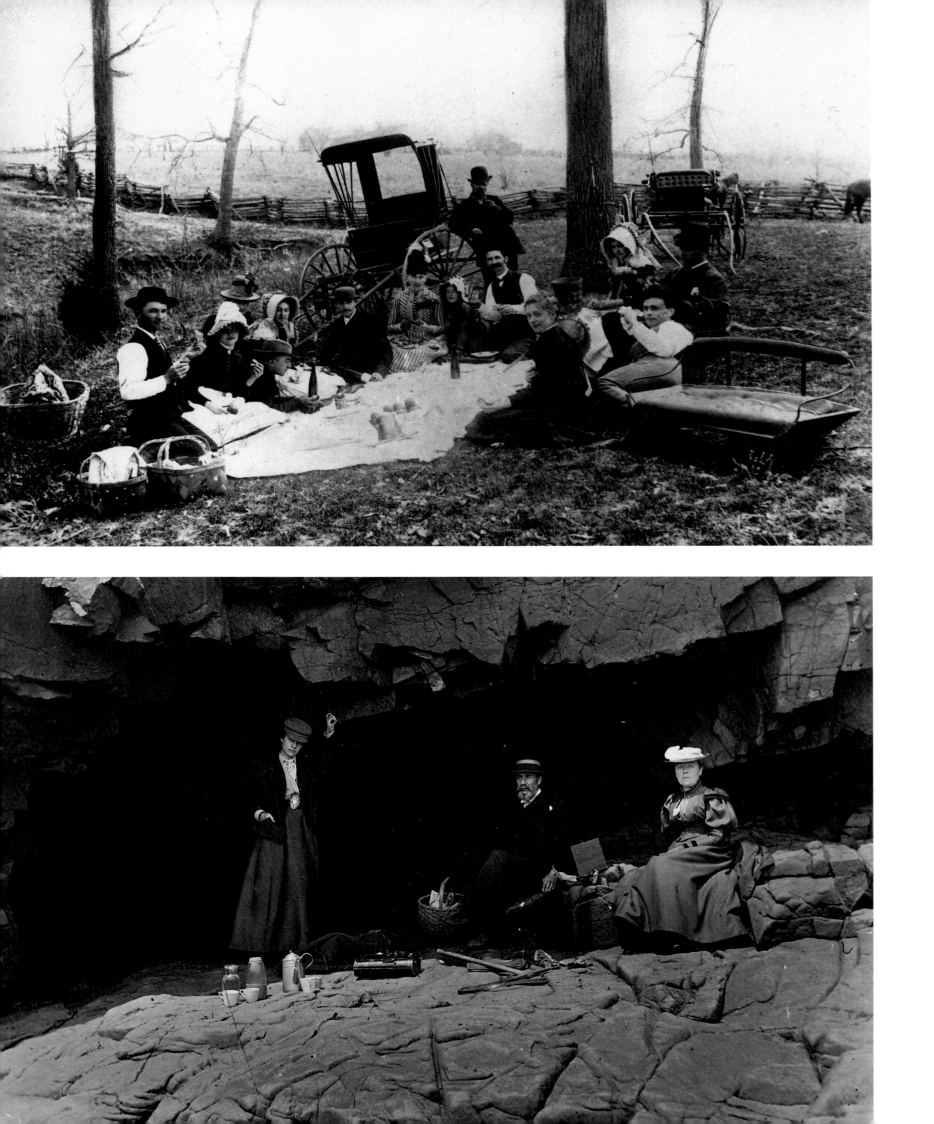

(OPPOSITE TOP) *Col. C.C. Bull and family, circa 1890, are enjoying themselves near Booneville, Missouri. The horses are off grazing and one of the carriage seats, empty at the moment, has become a plein air sofa.*

 (OPPOSITE BOTTOM) *Dressed rather formally and looking none too gay, this trio has nevertheless found an intriguing place for a picnic.*

 (BELOW) *People in the 1890s loved to be photographed munching watermelon in groups. This prime example shows a watermelon picnic in the Maine woods in August 1894.*

 (OPPOSITE) *An elderly gentleman, perched comfortably on a stump in 1895, fishes with a cane pole, while fully attired in a three-piece suit, boater, and even a watch chain.*

 (ABOVE) *A. S. Campbell of Elizabeth, New Jersey, photographed these ladies and gentlemen enjoying a quiet cruise in a swan boat on Central Park Lake.*

The New Olympians

When the modern Olympics began in Athens in 1896, they celebrated the rebirth of a tradition that had existed for more than a thousand years in ancient Greece. These new Olympics were the result of decades of discussion and planning by people from many countries, but a French baron is credited with being the games' principal proponent.

Pierre de Coubertin's devotion to the creation of a modern Olympics was inspired by his admiration for ancient Greek tradition, which maintained that human beings should strive for vitality in both mind and body and that sports were as important as intellectual activities. He was further stimulated by his tours of America and Britain, where, in the 1880s and 1890s, competitive sports were becoming increasingly important in educational institutions. He also found a general fever for sports in the cities of America, where athletic clubs and organizations were emerging as an integral part of urban life.

The modern games were considerably different than the old Olympics. Bicycle racing substituted for chariot races, and fencing for pugilism, and of course, the competitors came from many nations, whereas only Greeks had been allowed to compete in the ancient rites.

In 1896, participating nations included Denmark, England, German, France, Hungary, Switzerland, the United States and the host country, Greece. Although the small U.S. team had to endure a long ocean voyage and arrived just in time for the roll call, its members still won nine of the 12 events. James B. Connolly, a Harvard student, took the gold medal for the triple jump (the hop, step, and jump) and thereby became the first Olympic champion in more than 15 centuries.

The Greeks themselves had little success, but they won the event they most desired—the 42-kilometer marathon. That race commemorated the run made by a soldier of ancient Greece, who journeyed from the plains of Marathon to Athens with the news of an important victory in 490 B. C. When a young Greek competitor entered the stadium first in the 1896 marathon, 60,000 spectators from all over the world rose to their feet as one and erupted into happy pandemonium.

That kind of spirited enthusiasm has helped keep the modern Olympics alive, despite periodic political squabbles and boycotts. With the exception of the two World Wars, the games have been held every four years since 1896.

(ABOVE LEFT) *The founder of the modern Olympic Games, Baron de Coubertin.*

(ABOVE RIGHT) *Inside the stadium, guards await the arrival of the King and Queen of Greece at their royal box. The stadium was almost always full during the first modern Olympics.*

(OPPOSITE) *Why these long-skirted ladies decided to climb a tree is unknown but they appear to be glad that they did.*

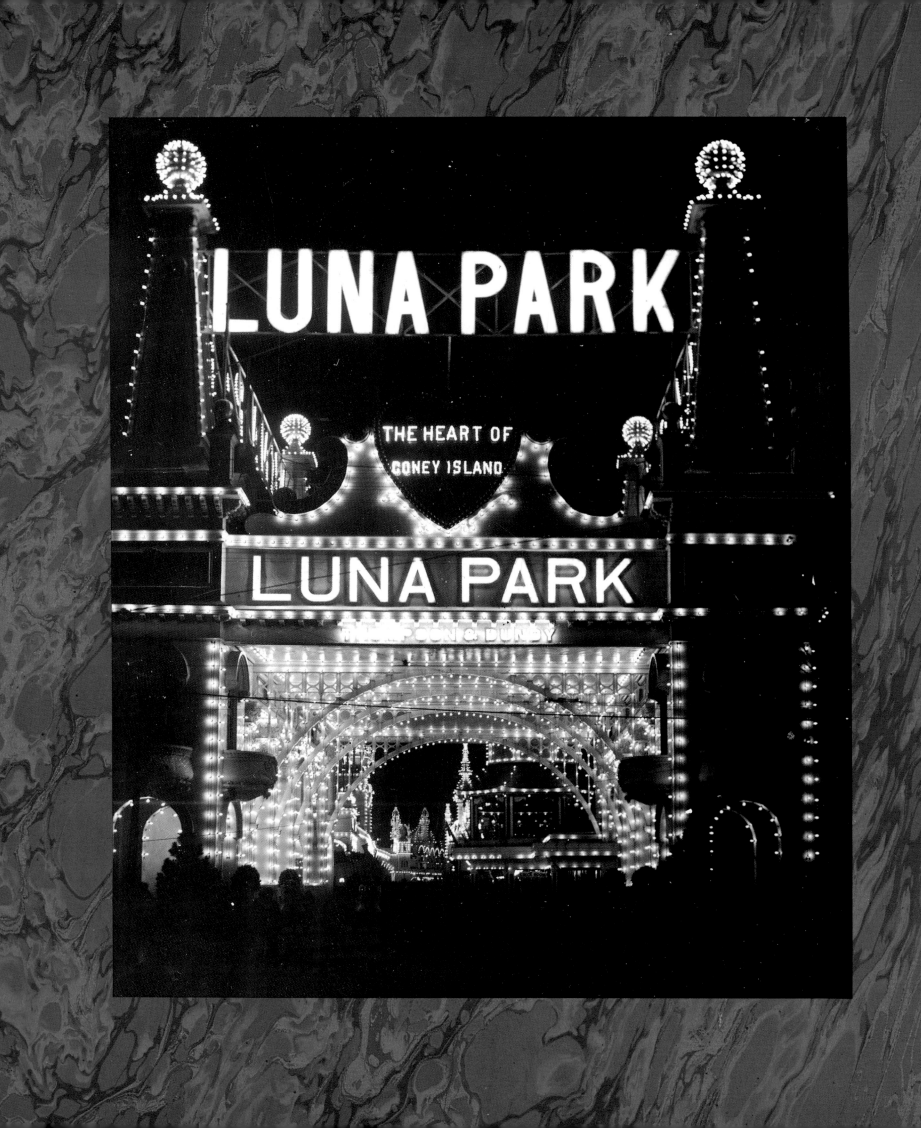

 (ABOVE) *"Ah there!" is the title of this "cheesecake" stereoptican photograph by Strohmeyer & Wyman. It was taken at Coney Island in 1897.*

 (RIGHT) **This stylish woman seems drawn to the hypnotic rhythms of the sea.**

(OPPOSITE) **Electric lights turned Luna Park, the fabulous Coney Island amusement park, into a magical place.**

Gentleman Jim Versus The Great John L.

Boxing grew up in the 1890s, changing from a bare-knuckle sport associated with law-breaking thugs and fakery to the "manly art" of three-minute rounds and padded gloves. The turning point came in 1892, when long-time bareknuckle champion John L. Sullivan fought a young newcomer nicknamed "Gentleman Jim" Corbett under the Marquis of Queensberry rules in New Orleans. That bout ended the reign of the Great John L., who had been heavyweight champion since 1882, when he won the last bareknuckle prizefight in the United States, a remarkable 75-round contest that lasted more than two hours.

The "Great John L." Sullivan was a hard-living Irish-American who represented a new kind of hero—urban-oriented, ethnic, and working class. He was the first of the great American sports figures to become known and loved by millions of ordinary people, a development made possible by the advent of a cohesive national press and a burgeoning communications network. By the late 1800s, every move he made was reported and—in Sullivan's opinion—exaggerated. However, John L's life-style made exaggeration unnecessary. He had a penchant for violent outbursts when drunk, he wasted enormous amounts of money on high living, and he beat his wife. Even though his excesses were often condemned, his strength and talent as a fighter were undeniable.

But boxing is a young man's game and when he took on the 26-year-old Corbett, Sullivan was overweight and looked ten years older than his 33 years. Corbett weighed 34 pounds less than Sullivan's 212, but he had speed, skill and finesse. The odds were on the champ, but the challenger stunned the world by knocking out the Great John L. in the 21st round. Corbett kept the championship until 1897, when he was beaten by Bob Fitzsimmons. For Sullivan, the fight was the end of an era. He tried desperately to stay in the public eye, performing in vaudeville and exhibition fights until his death in 1918. He never fought seriously again.

"Gentleman Jim" Corbett, 1897.

John L. Sullivan, 1882

 Baseball had enjoyed widespread popularity for several decades by the end of the 19th century. One of the heroes of the age was Hall of Famer Cap Anson, who played first base and managed the Chicago White Stockings during the 1890s. He batted .339 in his 22 years with the National League, and ended his career with 3,081 hits.

Between sledding, ice skating, and sleigh-riding, winter offered the 1890s fun-seeker a host of pleasures . . .

 (OPPOSITE) *Ice skating was almost too popular on the lake in Central Park.*

 (BELOW) *Sledding was the winter sport of choice on this New York hillside.*

 (RIGHT) *A rakish skipper and his two female companions take advantage of a windy summer day.*

 (OPPOSITE) *A debonair young man waits for the serve on a court in France, circa 1900.*

 (BELOW) *In 1899, the Columbia, one of the loveliest sailing yachts in New York harbor, met the British challenger, Shamrock I, for the America's Cup. Columbia won in three straight heats.*

Englishman James K. Starley introduced the modern bicycle in the late 1880s as a practical means of transportation. Soon people everywhere could be seen peddling through town and in the countryside. Indeed, the number of bikes in use climbed from 20,000 in 1882 to over 1 million in 1893 . . .

The Beginning of Basketball

It was a sport born of desperation. A physical education teacher with an incorrigible class was looking for a game of skill that could be played indoors during the winter with a minimum of body contact. He wrote down thirteen rules and used a couple of peach baskets for goals—and basketball was born. It was a success from the first impromptu game in 1891.

The inventor, Dr. James Naismith, was on the faculty of a training school for administrators of Young Men's Christian Associations in Springfield, Massachusettes (later Springfield College). The head of the physical education department, Dr. Luther Gulick, realized that his students were bored by many of the traditional winter activities as compared with the popular spring, summer, and fall sports like football and baseball. In addition, Gulick needed an instructor for a troublesome gym class of men who had already run through two teachers in the fall of 1891. He ordered Naismith to find a solution to this dual dilemma.

Naismith tried indoor variations on football, soccer and lacrosse, and was on the verge of admitting failure when he thought up the new game. After seeing its popularity, he selected nine men from his class and took them on an exhibition tour in 1892.

Soon women and girls were playing the game, too. Indeed, women's colleges like Vassar and Smith added basketball to their activities at the same time that the University of Chicago and Vanderbilt University established men's teams. During the remainder of the decade, college basketball expanded quickly and by 1900, Yale University was taking its team on the road, playing games in the Western states.

It would take many years and a prolonged effort to develop a single, universal code of basketball rules, and problems with violent contact between players would grow. Nonetheless, basketball was a solid success and never faltered after it was introduced in the 1890s.

 The first basketball team in Springfield, Massachusetts, 1891. The inventor of the game, Dr. James Naismith, is center row right.

 (LEFT) *Lord Stanley of Preston, the governor-general of Canada. The trophy that he donated in 1893 for the first amateur ice hockey championship in Canada has since become the sport's premier symbol of achievement for professionals.*

 (BELOW) *The team of the Montreal Amateur Athletic Assocation, winners of the first Stanley Cup.*

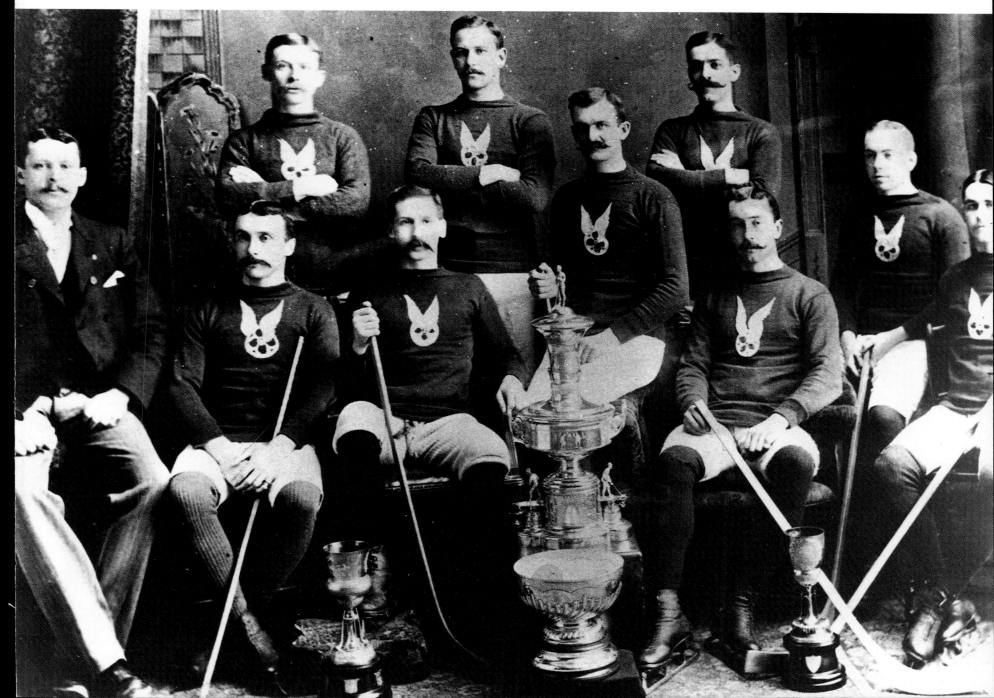

Five couples enjoy a bit of rest at West Barnet, Vermont, after a round of fishing. Their catch can be seen in the lower left portion of the picture.

PHOTO CREDITS

t = top, b = bottom, u.r. = upper right, u.l. = upper left, l.r. = lower right, l.l = lower left, l = left, c = center, r = right

The Academy of Motion Pictures Arts & Sciences 74 (b)
American Heritage Center, University of Wyoming 108, 139
Susan B. Anthony Memorial, Inc. 15
Arkansas History Commission 52 (t)
Atlanta Historical Society, Inc. 142 (b), 156-157, 158 (t)
Atwater-Kent Museum 160, 161 (t)
The Bancroft Library, University of California at Berkeley 66
Barker Texas History Center 101 (t)
Basketball Hall of Fame 190
The Bettmann Archive, Inc. 2, 3, 21 (u.r.), 22, 23 (u.r.), 24 (b), 25, 26 (l.r.), 28, 29 (b), 34 (t), 35 (b), 37, 39, 43, 48, 63 (t), 72 (b), 76, 77, 80, 84 (l.r.), 85 (u.l. & l.l.), 87, 89 (b), 114, 115 (b), 124, 126-127, 130- 131, 133, 135, 137 (r), 141 (t), 153, 154 (r), 155, 157 (r), 161 (b), 163, 166 (t), 168, 172 (t), 175, 176, 178 (l), 186 (b), 187, 188 (u.l. & b), 188- 189 (b), 189 (b)
Biltmore Estate 125 (t)
Buffalo Bill Ranch, North Patte, Nebraska 86 (b)
Chicago Historical Society 68
Colorado Historical Society 17 (l.l.), 34 (b), 69, 92 (b), 95 (b), 122 (l), 179
Culver Pictures, Inc. Front jacket, 8-9, 12 (b), 13, 16 (u.l., c, & u.r.), 17 (u.l., c, & u.r.), 21 (c), 23 (u.l.), 24 (t), 26 (l.l.), 27 (u.l. & l.r.), 29 (t), 31, 54 (t & b), 55 (u.l.), 56, 57 (t), 58, 59, 60 (b), 61, 62, 63 (b), 64, 65, 73, 75, 78, 79, 81, 86 (l.), 88, 90-91, 93 (t), 98 (t), 105, 107 (r), 117, 118 (b), 120, 121 (b), 132 (b), 133 (r), 140, 141 (b), 146, 148- 149, 150-151, 152, 153 (l.l.), 158 (b), 166 (b), 169 (l.l.), 174 (b), 178 (r), 181 (r), 182 (r), 186 (t), 189 (u.r.)
Historical Society of Delaware 123
Florida State Archives 16 (l.l. & l.r.), 17 (l.l.), 23 (b), 38 (b), 49 (b), 110-111, 170-171
Hawaii Historical Society 30
Hockey Hall of Fame 191
Idaho State Historical Society 106 (l), 173 (b)
Kentucky Historical Society 112 (b), 173 (t)
The Kobal Collection 55 (u.r.), 74 (c)
Library of Congress 10, 11, 12 (t), 14, 18 (l & r), 19, 20 (l, r, & u.r.), 21 (u.l.), 26 (u.r.), 27 (u.r. & l.l.), 51 (b), 72 (t), 74 (t), 84 (l.l.), 85 (r), 89 (t), 96, 112 (t), 113 (b), 115 (t), 116 (t), 118 (t), 119, 121 (t), 134 (t & b), 136, 137 (l), 145 (t), 147, 154 (l), 159, 162, 164, 169 (r), 172 (b), 181 (l), 185, 188-189 (t), 189 (u.l.)
Minnesota Historical Society 46, 67, 145 (b)
Mississippi Department of Archives and History 49 (t)
Missouri Historical Society 156, 174 (t)
Museum of New Mexico 95 (t)
Museum of the City of New York 57 (b), 184
National Archives 84 (u.l.), 92 (top), 93 (b), 101 (b), 103 (t), 104, 109, 132 (t)
National Baseball Library, Cooperstown, NY 183
National Park Service: Statue of Liberty National Monument 60 (t)
New York Public Library, Schomburg Center for Research in Black Studies 122 (r), 129 (l)
Oklahoma Historical Society 41, 44-45, 97 (b), 98 (b), 102-103 (b)
The Preservation Society of Newport County 125 (b)
Sears, Roebuck and Company 35 (t), 50
SuperStock 52-53, 68 (t), 83
Texas State Archives 94
Utah State Historical Society 32-33, 40, 70-71, 99, 100, 142 (t), 144, 165, 166-167
Vermont Historical Society 36 (b), 42, 47, 192
Western History Collection, University of Oklahoma Library 26 (u.l.)
State Historical Society of Wisconsin 38 (t)
Frank Lloyd Wright Foundation 116 (b)
Wyoming State Archives, Museum & Historical Department 97 (t)

ACKNOWLEDGEMENTS

The producers of *100 Years Ago: The Glorious 1890s* gratefully acknowledge the following individuals who assisted in the creation of this book:

Academy of Motion Picture Arts and Sciences, Margaret Herrick Library, Janet Lorenz; Arizona Historical Society, Deborah Shelton; Arkansas Historical Commission, Lynn Ewbank; Atlanta Historical Society, Ted Ryan; The Bancroft Library, University of California at Berkeley, Lawrence Dinnean; The Bethel Historical Society, Stanley Russell Howe; The Brooklyn Historical Society, Claire Marie Lamers; California Railroad Museum, Blaine Lamb; Chicago Historical Society, Linda Ziemer; Circus World Museum, Robert L. Parkinson; Colorado Historical Society, Becky Lintz; Dacus Library, Winthrop College, Ron Chepesiuk; Ellis Island Museum, Jeff Dosik; Flordia State Archives, Joanna Norman; George Eastman House, Janice Madhu; Hawaii State Archives, Susan Shaner; Henry Ford Museum and Greenfield Village, Cynthia Read-Miller; The Historical Society of Delaware, L. Ellen Peters; The Historical Society of Pennsylvania, Ellen Slack; Idaho State Historical Society, Elizabeth Jacox; Indiana Historical Society, Lisa Lussier; Kansas State Historical Society, Nancy Sherbert; Kentucky Historical Society, Mary Winter; Los Alamos Historical Museum, Theresa A. Strottman; Maine Historical Society, Elizabeth Singer Maule; Minnesota Historical Society, Dona Sieden; Mississippi Department of Archives and History, Elaine Owens; Missouri Historical Society, Jill Sherman; Musuem of the City of New York, Terry Ariano, Gretchen Viehmann; National Automotive History Collection, Detroit Public Library, Ron Grantz; National Museum of American History, Mary Grassick; The National Portrait Gallery, Smithsonian Institution, Patricia Svoboda; Nevada Historical Society, Erik Lauritzen; New Mexico State Archives, Arthur Olivas; New York Public Library, Schomburg Center for Research in Black Culture, Jim Huffman; Newport Historical Society, Elliott Caldwell; Ohio Historical Society, Tauni Graham; Oklahoma Historical Society; Oregon Historical Society, Jean Elkington; The Preservation Society of Newport County, Monique Panaggio; Society for the Preservation of New England Antiquities, Lorna Condon; South Carolina Historical Society, Mary Giles; South Dakota Historical Society, Ann Jenks; Stanford University Archives, Stephen Mandeville-Gamble; State Historical Society of Wisconsin, Myrna Williamson; State of New Mexico State Records and Archives, Ron Montoya; Susan B. Anthony House, Roberta LaChiusa; Texas State Library, John Anderson; United States Naval Academy Museum, Jane Price; University of Chicago Library, Elizabeth Sage; University of Chicago Special Collections, Daniel Meyer; University of Illinois at Chicago, Mary Ann Bamberger; University of Oklahoma, John Lovett; Utah State Historical Society, Susan Whetstone; Vermont Historical Society, Mary Pat Brigham; Virginia Historical Society, Laurie Horner; Virginia State Library and Archives, Mark Scala; Wyoming State Archives, Museum and Historical Department, Paula Chavoya.